"Mitchell Chase takes readers on a journey ... the rich concept of wisdom. In the process, he helps us develop a well-rounded understanding of biblical wisdom. The numerous applications in this book show us what wise living can look like in life's varied circumstances and that biblical theology is relevant to the life of the church and the believer. Those who want to be numbered among the wise who 'shine . . . like the stars' (Dan 12:3) in our fallen world will surely benefit from this book."

Kevin Chen, professor of Old Testament studies at Gateway Seminary in Ontario, California

"Mitchell Chase is one of my favorite readers of Scripture. He pays close attention to the Spirit-inspired text, reads every text in light of the biblical story and its culmination in the person and work of Christ, and sheds light on how every text is written for the instruction of the people of God in every day and age. *Walking the Way of the Wise* is the latest example, and I highly recommend it. Readers will be encouraged, comforted, and challenged!"

Matthew Y. Emerson, academic dean and coprovost at Oklahoma Baptist University

"Biblical theologians sensitive to the narrative arc of Holy Scripture sometimes find difficulty plotting the so-called 'wisdom literature.' In this excellent book, pastor-theologian Mitchell Chase demonstrates that the theme of wisdom, concentrated in that particular corpus, dovetails naturally with the broader biblical storyline and many other important biblical motifs. 'Where shall wisdom be found?' Job asks. The biblical reflections in this book go a long way toward answering that perennial human question."

R. Lucas Stamps, professor of Christian theology at Clamp Divinity School at Anderson University

"In *Walking the Way of the Wise*, Mitchell Chase traces and interconnects the wisdom theme throughout the biblical story, demonstrating that wise living is a foundational and character-defining feature of the life that God's people are called to live. This book is strong academically, but it is also very readable and engaging, even enriching to one's own personal walk with God. I highly recommend it."

J. Daniel Hays, professor of biblical studies at Ouachita Baptist University

"'Get wisdom,' spoken by a king who could not live up to his own ideals, is easier said than done. Thankfully, there is a greater-than-Solomon King who reveals wisdom through his cross and gives it by his Spirit. In *Walking the Way of the Wise*, pastor-scholar Mitchell Chase guides his readers through the storyline of Scripture, examining the parts in light of the whole, to help them know and enjoy Christ, in whom all the treasures of wisdom and knowledge are found. So take up, read, and walk wisely in Christ!"

Oren R. Martin, equipping pastor at Providence Church and associate professor of Christian theology at The Southern Baptist Theological Seminary and Boyce College

WALKING THE WAY OF THE WISE
A Biblical Theology of Wisdom

MITCHELL L. CHASE

An imprint of InterVarsity Press
Downers Grove, Illinois

InterVarsity Press
P.O. Box 1400 | Downers Grove, IL 60515-1426
ivpress.com | email@ivpress.com

©2025 by Mitchell Loyd Chase

All rights reserved. No part of this book may be reproduced in any form without written permission from InterVarsity Press.

InterVarsity Press® is the publishing division of InterVarsity Christian Fellowship/USA®. For more information, visit intervarsity.org.

Scripture quotations, unless otherwise noted, are from The Holy Bible, English Standard Version, copyright © 2001 by Crossway Bibles, a division of Good News Publishers. Used by permission. All rights reserved.

The publisher cannot verify the accuracy or functionality of website URLs used in this book beyond the date of publication.

Cover design: Faceout Studio
Interior design: Daniel van Loon
Image: © Shomiz / DigitalVision Vectors via Getty Images

ISBN 978-1-5140-1091-4 (print) | ISBN 978-1-5140-1092-1 (digital)

Printed in the United States of America ∞

Library of Congress Cataloging-in-Publication Data
Names: Chase, Mitchell L., 1983- author.
Title: Walking the way of the wise : a biblical theology of wisdom / Mitchell L. Chase.
Description: Downers Grove, IL : IVP Academic, [2025] | Series: Essential studies in biblical theology | Includes bibliographical references and index.
Identifiers: LCCN 2024047320 (print) | LCCN 2024047321 (ebook) | ISBN 9781514010914 (paperback) | ISBN 9781514010921 (ebook)
Subjects: LCSH: Wisdom–Biblical teaching. | Bible–Theology.
Classification: LCC BS680.W6 C43 2025 (print) | LCC BS680.W6 (ebook) | DDC 223–dc23/eng/20250108
LC record available at https://lccn.loc.gov/2024047320
LC ebook record available at https://lccn.loc.gov/2024047321

For my friend Caleb Dye,

who helps me run the race

with greater joy.

CONTENTS

Series Preface | *ix*

Acknowledgments | *xi*

Introduction | *1*

  1 The Knowledge of Good and Evil | *7*

  2 Righteous Suffering and Spiritual Warfare | *21*

  3 Walking the Path Toward Inheritance | *32*

  4 What Was Right in Their Own Eyes | *49*

  5 Singing with a Choir of Witnesses | *61*

  6 Wisdom for Royal Sons and Daughters | *74*

  7 Covenant Love for Covenant People | *89*

  8 A Fleeting Life Under the Sun | *101*

  9 Following Lady Folly into Exile | *117*

  10 Something Greater Than Solomon | *130*

  11 Walking Wisely in Evil Days | *142*

  12 The End of the Narrow Way | *155*

Discussion Guide | *163*

Scripture Index | *165*

SERIES PREFACE

L. MICHAEL MORALES

BIBLICAL THEOLOGY HAS SURELY ENTERED a spring season, causing all who love the Scriptures to rejoice in the beauty and strength of its array of blossoms. Happily, since the original Essential Studies in Biblical Theology has proven to be a particularly ripe vine, IVP Academic has extended its publication for another round of volumes in the series, in good hope of further fruit.

From the dozens of dissertations coming out of biblical studies departments, and technical monographs of established scholars, down to weekly ministry-related blogposts, the increasing output of works of biblical theology has continued unabated. Nevertheless, the special features of the ESBT series, which led to its popularity, remain unique and ensure its vital place and contribution. ESBT has found that superb and extremely difficult balance of canon-wide exegesis and a warm, lay-level tone—solid scholarship for the church's delight.

For this second round of ESBT volumes, therefore, readers can expect an offering of major themes, purveyed in the full sweep of redemptive history, from Eden (Gen 1–3) to the new Jerusalem (Rev 21–22). Once more, sound scholarship will be wed to accessibility, both in terms of writing style and the relatively brief length of each volume. With skillful attention to nuanced development, authors will unfold their subjects in relation to the advent of the Messiah, the person and work of the Lord Jesus, and with an eye to practical application for the people of God in today's world. Our sincere hope and prayer is that these further volumes will encourage every reader not only to grasp the story and message of the Scriptures more deeply, finding his or her own place within its story, but to know, love, and adore the triune God of the Bible, and so to serve him with greater joy and gladness.

ACKNOWLEDGMENTS

WRITING A BOOK IS TEAMWORK. There is the initial back-and-forth about ideas and structure and direction that precedes a manuscript. There is the mental dialogue with books and articles that stimulate insights and clarity. There is the recognition that what you write is the downstream result of upstream influences that have shaped you. There is the support system that keeps a project's momentum going—a support system consisting of the writer's publisher and the writer's household.

I've been blessed with a splendid team, and that has made this project a delight to write. I'm thankful for Michael Morales, who exhibited interest and enthusiasm in the project from its inception. I've benefited so much from his scholarship over the years, and it's been an honor to have his attentive eye on this manuscript. I love the Essential Studies in Biblical Theology series, so I'm humbled by InterVarsity Press's warm welcome of a volume on a biblical theology of wisdom. I want to acknowledge Rachel Hastings, my academic editor, whose support, time, and comments have helped this project along the narrow way that leads to publication.

As a professor at Boyce College and The Southern Baptist Theological Seminary, I'm eager for students to learn and love the Old and New

Testaments. And as the preaching pastor at Kosmosdale Baptist Church in Louisville, I'm eager for church members to grow in their understanding of and commitment to Scripture. My prayer is that all the learning and study, in every setting, will lead to deeper joy and hope in God—and especially the fear of the Lord.

This book is dedicated to Caleb Dye, my friend and fellow church elder. I'm glad to serve in ministry with him, and I'm thankful he's literally my neighbor. Having known Caleb for more than a decade, I've seen the Lord's gracious work in his life. Caleb desires to fear the Lord and walk in wisdom. He pursues the kind of life that the book of Proverbs commends.

At the completion of this manuscript, my four boys are fifteen, thirteen, eleven, and seven years old. The soundtrack for much of this book has been their lively presence in our home. I wouldn't have it any other way. My dear wife, Stacie, is my best friend and my favorite reader. She read through a draft of this book to give thoughtful feedback, and I'm always amazed how she finds the time. As in our home, so also with this project: she makes everything better.

INTRODUCTION

"WHAT DO YOU WANT TO BE when you grow up?" Someone probably asked you that question, more than once. It is fascinating to hear the dreams of being a professional athlete or an astronaut or a famous inventor. While I do not know the correspondence between a child's answer and the actual adult vocation, I imagine that more often than not the child's answer was different from what came to pass.

The question "What do you want to be?" is typically interpreted as vocational. When adults ask children that question, they mean it in a vocational sense. But let's deepen the question and make it a bit longer: "What *kind of person* do you want to be when you grow up?" This question is good for children to think about, and it is good for adults too.

PEOPLE WHO CHANGE

We are becoming certain kinds of people. Humans are not static beings. We grow, we are influenced by others, and we are affected by circumstances. You are not who you once were, and you are not who you will be.

For Christians, the reality of change is even more profound. God has done a merciful work that has fundamentally changed us, and he is not finished.

If we are in Christ, we are a new creation (2 Cor 5:17). This spiritual truth carries both earthly and eternal ramifications. We are inwardly being renewed (2 Cor 4:16), and our future is a weight of glory consisting of resurrection life (2 Cor 4:17–5:5). God has begun a good work in us, and he will bring it to completion (Phil 1:6).

God's good work empowers Christian growth, and growing in Christ involves growing in wisdom. What do you want to be when you grow up? "Wise" is a great answer, maybe even the best answer. Wisdom in the biblical sense is more than street smarts. It is more than cleverness in a particular field. Biblical wisdom is the result of living in glad submission to God's Word in God's world. Biblical wisdom is believing what God has revealed and seeking to live in light of it.

Do you want to be wise? Do you want to understand what the biblical authors teach about this topic that affects your life at a deep level?

MORE THAN SIX BOOKS

Biblical wisdom is a whole-Bible subject. This might surprise readers who think of wisdom as something that only a small number of Old and New Testament books address.[1] If you were to ask which biblical books are about wisdom, a common answer would name Job, Proverbs, and Ecclesiastes. Three books. If someone named more books than these, they might add some psalms, the Song of Songs, and the letter of James, totaling six books.

Now, it is true that these books teach wisdom, but what if biblical wisdom involves more than these six? What if we were open to wisdom as primarily a concept rather than primarily a genre?[2] A genre is about similarities in form and style. And because the three—or six—books mentioned above

---

[1] Our study will not explore apocryphal books, such as Ecclesiasticus or the Wisdom of Solomon.
[2] For the past couple of hundred years, scholars have referred to "Wisdom literature." In *An Obituary for "Wisdom Literature": The Birth, Death, and Intertextual Integration of a Biblical Corpus* (New York: Oxford University Press, 2019), Will Kynes traces the rise of this language and the influence of Johann Bruch. Kynes pushes back against the popular notion that "wisdom" is a kind of genre. Kynes writes, "I propose understanding the definition of wisdom as a concept broadly, based on the role of the concept and the diverse traits associated with it in the variety of texts in which they appear, and not necessarily united in a singular distinct worldview. . . . This, in effect, would treat wisdom (now with a lowercase 'W') as a concept, similar to 'holiness' or 'righteousness,' instead of as a genre, movement, or tradition" (252-53).

Introduction

contain things such as poetic structure, parallelisms, proverbial statements, and/or lengthy discourses instructing the recipients in wisdom, "Wisdom literature" is common language among scholars. While noting a book's genre(s) can shed interpretive light on the passages therein, a danger also exists. We should not use the concept of genre to exclude the presence of complex literary styles or features in a book. For instance, have you noticed that there are prophecies in Genesis, a book outside the so-called Prophets? Have you seen the narrative bookends of Job's story, even though poetry is the dominant style in the intervening chapters?

In order to understand what the biblical authors teach about wisdom, we must not limit our focus to the so-called Wisdom books. Job, Psalms, Proverbs, Ecclesiastes, the Song of Songs, and James are crucial books for the subject at hand, and we will engage them in due course, but biblical wisdom is a concern in the whole Bible. I am not arguing that everything in Scripture is wisdom; if everything is wisdom, then nothing is. But there are plenty of places outside the "Wisdom literature" that serve to instruct people in how to think and live in God's world. In some passages that teach us how to live wisely, the word *wisdom* is not even used. Therefore, an effort to understand wisdom in the Bible must be more than a word study and more than a focus on a recognized set of books.

Is the phrase "Wisdom literature" worth retaining, especially if wisdom is better called a concept? Are there "wisdom books" in the Bible? Tremper Longman notes, "Genres are not rigid and pure. Texts do not have one and only one genre, but can be part of different literary groupings that illuminate the individual text. Genres have fuzzy boundaries. It is with this understanding of genre that we believe it is appropriate to describe a wisdom genre in the Bible." What would be a key—or *the* key—element in identifying a so-called wisdom genre? Again, Longman: "The main identifier of the wisdom genre is simply that these texts are interested in the concept of wisdom."[3] And there are particular books in Scripture—such as Job, Proverbs, and Ecclesiastes—that are so dominated by the concept of wisdom, by way of structure and content and purpose, that calling them "Wisdom literature" seems fitting.

---

[3] Tremper Longman III, *The Fear of the Lord Is Wisdom: A Theological Introduction to Wisdom in Israel* (Grand Rapids, MI: Baker Academic, 2017), 281.

If we are going to explore what the Bible teaches about wisdom, we will also welcome passages of various genres, passages that point us to wisdom and life, passages that show the blessings of obedience and the consequences of folly.

THE STORY LINE CHALLENGE

There are biblical themes discernible along the storyline of Scripture, such as the themes of temple or priesthood or sacrifice or exodus or sonship. As we trace progressive revelation in the writings of the biblical authors, these themes develop. These themes not only find greater clarity across the canon, but they meet in and escalate toward the splendid revelation of Christ's person and work.

The theme of wisdom is not so obvious along the Bible's story line. But we must remember that the biblical authors both show *and* tell. The narratives teach biblical truth in ways different from propositional claims or proverbial statements. A biblical theology of wisdom must notice how the different biblical genres showcase wisdom.

Since wisdom may not seem to advance the story line of Scripture, the theme can suffer neglect as other good and important themes occupy the attention of readers and interpreters. We will be wise to correct any imbalance.

The task of biblical theology is interested in how the various parts of Scripture correspond to the whole, how things fit together in the grand scheme of God's redemptive purposes. Therefore, a discussion of wisdom must incorporate elements such as the fear of the Lord, the trees in the midst of the garden, the binary paths of blessing and curse, the covenants, the national experience of Israel, the ministry of the Lord Jesus, the ethics for new covenant life, and the consummation at Christ's second advent.

Let me put a map in your hand. The subsequent chapters follow a salvation-historical trajectory.

Chapter 1 roots us in the early chapters of Scripture, where the seeds—and even a tree—of wisdom are found. Chapter 2 discusses the story and person of Job, since I think his life was very early in biblical history. With chapters 3 and 4, we follow the stories and steps of Abraham and his descendants—the Israelites. In chapter 5 we see the rise of David and we hear his songs, his psalms. The shadow of Solomon looms over chapters 6, 7, and 8, as we reflect on his life and on the books of Proverbs, the Song of Songs, and Ecclesiastes. Our exploration of wisdom in the Old Testament concludes with chapter 9, where we follow the Israelites into exile, which is where folly takes its disciples. Chapter 10 directs our attention to the incarnation and ministry of Jesus, the true and greater Solomon. In chapter 11 we consider the importance of walking wisely as Christ's people, for the days are evil. And finally, in chapter 12, we cast our eyes toward the end of the wise road—the way that leads to life and blessing, the life we were made and saved for.

This salvation-historical trajectory will help us situate Scripture's teaching about wisdom in light of the big story of Scripture itself. With a canonical perspective on wisdom, we will see the various ways that the biblical authors instruct us about this topic. And we will more fully appreciate how they summon us to join the blessed and joyful saints who are walking the way of the wise.

Chapter One

THE KNOWLEDGE OF GOOD AND EVIL

THE OPENING CHAPTERS OF GENESIS contain foundational and consequential events. We encounter the truth that God is the Creator, who used nothing to create everything. He is the one who speaks light, parts water, fills land, and declares things "good." We read of an ordered world. Evening and morning are followed by another evening and morning, and so on to this very day.

As the story progresses, the biblical author tells of a plot to undermine God's good design, to bring havoc into his good world. Lies echo in sacred space, and image bearers choose folly instead of wisdom.

ORDER IN THE WORLD

In Genesis 1:26, God says, "Let us make man in our image, after our likeness. And let them have dominion over the fish of the sea and over the birds of the heavens and over the livestock and over all the earth and over every creeping thing that creeps on the earth." God made humans male and female (Gen 1:27), and he blessed them with the instruction, "Be fruitful and multiply and fill the earth and subdue it, and have dominion over the fish of the sea and over the birds of the heavens and over every living thing that moves on the earth" (Gen 1:28).

The language in Genesis 1:28 echoes Genesis 1:26, which means that part of being an image bearer is representing God's rule in the world. It is the task of exercising dominion, of subduing creation. Like an ancient Near Eastern king might install his royal image in a land to claim it for his name and realm, God has placed his royal images in the world he has made.[1] Placing image bearers in his world is a signal of his divine ownership, and at the same time, being an image bearer involves subduing the world owned by God.

God's creation in Genesis 1, and his task to his image bearers in Genesis 1:28, brims with order and design. As Proverbs 3:19-20 says, "The LORD by wisdom founded the earth; by understanding he established the heavens; by his knowledge the deeps broke open, and the clouds drop down the dew." He makes light and separates it from darkness (Gen 1:4). He separates waters (Gen 1:9). He brings forth land (Gen 1:9-10) from the waters, and on it he forms plants and fruit trees (Gen 1:11-12). A rhythm of "evening and morning" moves from one day to the next.

The Lord causes living creatures to fill the waters and the skies (Gen 1:20). He commands the living creatures, "Be fruitful and multiply and fill the waters in the seas, and let birds multiply on the earth" (Gen 1:22). This language in Genesis 1:22 echoes in the commission to image bearers in Genesis 1:26 and Genesis 1:28. But there is a crucial difference. While the animals will procreate, they will not have dominion over God's image bearers. Only humankind exists in the image of God, and only God's image bearers will subdue the created order. Desmond Alexander is right: "Through commissioning human beings to govern all land animals, birds and fish, God sets them apart from all other creatures and gives them a royal status."[2]

Reflecting on the events and movement throughout Genesis 1, we notice order and design. We see human beings as the climax of God's creative work,

---

[1] See Peter J. Gentry and Stephen J. Wellum, *Kingdom Through Covenant: A Biblical-Theological Understanding of the Covenants*, 2nd ed. (Wheaton, IL: Crossway, 2018), 220-38.

[2] T. Desmond Alexander, *From Eden to the New Jerusalem: An Introduction to Biblical Theology* (Grand Rapids, MI: Kregel Academic, 2008), 76. He says, "The concept of royalty underlies the expression 'image of God.' In the ancient Near East, in both Egypt and Mesopotamia, the phrase 'image of God' was commonly linked to kings. The king was the living 'image of a god'" (76).

and we read of these image bearers receiving the commission to exercise dominion and to subdue creatures and creation. Since God is the author of creation and the supreme authority in the world, whatever he says is good. His commands direct his image bearers in what is good. The goodness of divine commands derives from the goodness of divine character.

How does wisdom factor into all this? Submission to our sovereign and good Creator is good and thus wise. If God has ordered the world in a certain way, and if he has given commands that direct the hearts and lives of his image bearers in a certain way, then defying God's design is foolishness. Wisdom would involve living according to God's design and commands, and foolishness would involve living contrary to them.

A FORBIDDEN TREE

When God makes his image bearers, he makes Adam first. He places the man in the garden (Gen 2:8), and in the midst of this garden are two trees. Plenty of trees were pleasing to the sight and good for food, but two trees are distinct: the tree of life and the tree of the knowledge of good and evil.

The Lord puts Adam in the garden to *work* it and *keep* it (Gen 2:15)—a pair of verbs that, when occurring together later in the Pentateuch, connect to priestly activity (Num 3:7-8; 8:26; 18:5-6).[3] More than a farmer, Adam is a priest in Eden. He is to work (or serve) the sacred space and keep (or guard) the vicinity.

A prohibition informs Adam about the trees in the garden. The Lord says, "You may surely eat of every tree of the garden, but of the tree of the knowledge of good and evil you shall not eat, for in the day that you eat of it you shall surely die" (Gen 2:16-17). One tree is off limits. And the prohibition comes with a consequence, a promise of something Adam does not have experience with: death.

The very name of the forbidden tree—"the tree of the knowledge of good and evil"—invokes terms we associate with wisdom. The wise discern between good and evil. Would image bearers not be helped by knowing good and evil so that they could love the former and abhor the latter?

---

[3]See G. K. Beale, *The Temple and the Church's Mission: A Biblical Theology of the Dwelling Place of God*, New Studies in Biblical Theology (Downers Grove, IL: InterVarsity Press, 2004), 66-70.

While the prohibition is a serious command, we would be overreading it if we were to conclude that the tree itself was bad or evil. God did not place an evil tree next to a good tree ("the tree of life") in the garden. Instead, *everything* God made was good. Perhaps the prohibition would only persist for a period of growth and testing, where God's image bearers would learn to trust the Lord and demonstrate obedience. Perhaps God would have eventually permitted his people to eat from this tree that had been for a time forbidden by him. If some kind of probationary period was in view, then trusting the Lord's prohibition would involve growth in wisdom, and this growth would lead to eating from the tree of the knowledge of good and evil at the appointed time. Even if such eating was possible at a later and divinely revealed time, the label of the tree might designate it as a judgment tree. "In this respect," says G. K. Beale, "the tree in Eden seems to have functioned as a judgment tree, the place where Adam should have gone to 'discern between good and evil' and, thus, where he should have judged the serpent as evil and pronounced judgment on it, as it entered the garden."[4]

In fact, let's talk about that serpent.

DISORDER IN THE GARDEN

Near the end of Genesis 2, the Lord makes the woman and brings her to the man (Gen 2:20-23). As male and female, they would fulfill the commission to be fruitful and multiply, and they would subdue God's creatures and creation because they—and not the animals in the sky or land or waters—existed as image bearers.

It is clear in the exchange between the woman and the serpent in Genesis 3 that she is already aware of the forbidden tree as well as the consequence if someone eats from it. Either the Lord told her directly or Adam told her directly, but the biblical narrative does not report how or when she knew.

At the beginning of Genesis 3, we read of a serpent in the garden of God. Here is a creeping thing, the likes of which we have read about in Genesis 1:25 ("everything that creeps on the ground"). Here, then, is a thing to subdue. So we wait to see whether an exercise of dominion is in store. But before

---

[4] G. K. Beale, *A New Testament Biblical Theology: The Unfolding of the Old Testament in the New* (Grand Rapids, MI: Baker Academic, 2011), 35.

that outcome is clear, we read a description: "the serpent was more crafty than any other beast of the field" (Gen 3:1). The language of craftiness is about shrewdness, and shrewdness is related to the concept of wisdom. Clearly the serpent is not wise in a God-honoring sense. But the serpent is clever and knows how to use words. The serpent manipulates, deceives, and tempts.

The serpent engages the woman with a question: "Did God actually say, 'You shall not eat of any tree in the garden'?" (Gen 3:1). If we recall the specifics of God's prohibition from Genesis 2:16-17, we realize that the serpent is distorting what God said. The serpent is portraying God as someone who created all these trees and who then denied them to his people. The serpent is telling a lie that distorts God's character and intent.

She corrects the serpent and says, "We may eat of the fruit of the trees of the garden, but God said, 'You shall not eat of the fruit of the tree that is in the midst of the garden, neither shall you touch it, lest you die'" (Gen 3:2-3). The language of "touch" is not in the original command (Gen 2:16-17), so some interpreters have concluded that she has wrongfully added to God's words. Others suspect that she says "touch" because touching the fruit would be necessary in order to eat it, and thus her words would be reasonable and not necessarily a distortion of God's command. Perhaps significant in this discussion is that neither in Genesis 3, nor in any later biblical passage, is there an indictment against the woman for what she says in Genesis 3:2-3 to the serpent.

What should stand out for the reader is the serpent's response in Genesis 3:4-5: "You will not surely die. For God knows that when you eat of it your eyes will be opened, and you will be like God, knowing good and evil." The creature is explicitly rejecting the warning God gave. The woman mentioned the threat of death (Gen 3:3), but the serpent says, "You will not surely die."

A stunning exchange is taking place in the sacred space of Eden's garden. A serpent is casting doubt on divine words. And while he is not exactly telling the woman to eat from the forbidden tree, he is portraying the divine command as impotent and the God who gave the command as withholding something important ("God knows . . . you will be like God," Gen 3:5).

The serpent has distorted God's words (Gen 3:1), questioned the seriousness of God's warning (Gen 3:4), and framed God's motive as stingy and selfish (Gen 3:5). When the woman reflects on the tree, she sees that the tree is good for food, a delight to the eyes, and desirable "to make one wise" (Gen 3:6). This last description—"to make one wise"—is the narrator's confirmation of what the "knowledge of good and evil" would bring. It would bring wisdom, because biblical wisdom distinguishes between what is right and what is wrong, what is good and what is evil.

But if God has forbidden the tree, then deciding to eat its fruit—even with the noble goal of getting wisdom—would be an *un*wise act. The serpent has portrayed God's words as misleading, yet it is the serpent who has spoken the misleading words. Wisdom is not acquired by rejecting God's commands but by submitting to them. In an act of defiance, the woman takes of the tree's fruit and eats, and she gives some to her husband, who is there with her, and he eats too (Gen 3:6). She does this because she believes what the serpent said, even though she knows what God said. Did Adam hear the whole conversation between the serpent and the woman? The narrator says he "was with her" when she gave him the fruit. So even though he knows what God has said, he too defies the divine command and follows the wrong initiative of his wife.

The whole scene in Genesis 3 brims with disorder.[5] Rather than subduing the serpent, the woman falls into deception, and Adam follows her into sin. They fail to exercise dominion over the creeping thing. The creeping thing exercises dominion over them! By inverting the created order, the serpent brings chaos not only into the garden but also into the relationship between Adam and Eve and in their relationship with God. The serpent approached the woman with his twisted words. Adam did not protect his wife, Eve did not trust the Lord, and neither Adam nor Eve subdued the vile creature who raised his words against God's goodness and command.

"Then the eyes of both were opened, and they knew that they were naked" (Gen 3:7).

---

[5] For a book-length treatment of Gen 3 and its role and echoes in subsequent biblical revelation, see Mitchell L. Chase, *Short of Glory: A Biblical and Theological Exploration of the Fall* (Wheaton, IL: Crossway, 2023).

OPEN EYES AND A CLOSED DOOR

The serpent's words had promised a desirable knowledge—"you will be like God, knowing good and evil" (Gen 3:5)—and so we must evaluate the actual result of the couple's action. We know they felt shame at their nakedness and vulnerability, because they sewed fig leaves together to cover themselves (Gen 3:7). They hid from the Lord when they heard his presence among them (Gen 3:8). And when the Lord questioned what they did, Adam pointed to his wife, and she pointed to the serpent (Gen 3:12-13).

Their "open eyes" do not quite bring the experience of godlikeness that the serpent promised (Gen 3:5). Though earlier naked and not ashamed, they are now naked and ashamed (Gen 2:25; 3:7, 10). They seized the fruit and, in doing so, reached for moral autonomy as well.[6] The narrative shows that the pursuit of moral autonomy is foolish. The ensuing consequences that God pronounced (in Gen 3:14-19) confirm the foolishness of the couple's actions, and the consequences confirm the deceptiveness of the serpent's words.

Before God exiles the couple from the Garden of Eden, he says, "Behold, the man has become like one of us in knowing good and evil" (Gen 3:22). At first glance, the Lord seems to be agreeing with what the serpent told the woman ("you will be like God, knowing good and evil," Gen 3:5). But in the context of Genesis 3, this "knowledge" has resulted in shame and seclusion. While the man and woman now have a greater sense of right and wrong, they gained this knowledge *through sin*. Instead of trusting God's goodness and timing, they seized moral autonomy and committed evil.

Having eaten from the forbidden tree, they will not be able to eat from the tree of life. The exile from Eden ensures that the man will not "take also of the tree of life and eat, and live forever" (Gen 3:22). The biblical narrative in Genesis 2 does not report whether the man or woman had eaten from the tree of life at any point. The Lord had not forbidden that tree, but exile will now make such eating impossible.

---

[6] According to Longman, "By eating the fruit of the tree, Adam and Eve are not gaining new information; they rather arrogate to themselves rather than to God the right to define moral categories. God has told them it was wrong to eat of the fruit, but in the act of eating it, they reject God's authority and assert their own right to determine what is right and what is wrong." Tremper Longman III, *The Fear of the Lord Is Wisdom: A Theological Introduction to Wisdom in Israel* (Grand Rapids, MI: Baker Academic, 2017), 95.

Unpermitted eating was foolish, and foolishness brought destruction and exile. The Lord drives the man east of the garden (Gen 3:24), and we are right to assume that the woman—whom Adam names Eve (Gen 3:20)—goes into exile too. The narrative of Genesis 1–3 intertwines the ideas of obedience and blessing, but it also intertwines rebellion and judgment. Wisdom and life go together; foolishness and death go together.

In order to close the entrance to the garden, God appoints cherubim, complete with a flaming sword, to guard the way to the tree of life (Gen 3:24). Ironically, the cherubim will guard the garden because the man failed to do so. Physical alienation from Eden symbolizes the deeper problem that sin and folly cause. The fool chooses his own way and rejects God's way. Such folly leads to destruction. And how could it not? If God is the source of all goodness and life, then a rejection of wisdom will reap the opposite of goodness and life.

THE FOLLY OF THE FIRST SON

Everyone who was ever born was born outside Eden. With the commission to be fruitful and multiply (Gen 1:28), Adam and Eve bear children. Each birth is into a fallen world where the presence of sin and corruption will be manifest. The problem of sin affects not only Adam and Eve but also their descendants.

The first two children are Cain and Abel, and in the course of time, each brings an offering to the Lord (Gen 4:1-4). The Lord receives Abel's offering, but he rejects Cain's. He tells Cain, "Why are you angry, and why has your face fallen? If you do well, will you not be accepted? And if you do not do well, sin is crouching at the door. Its desire is contrary to you, but you must rule over it" (Gen 4:6-7).

Nowhere in God's words to Cain does the term *wisdom* appear. But the Lord is certainly exhorting Cain to wisdom and away from folly. Sin is like a predator, crouching and biding its time, waiting for the opportune moment to jump and conquer. If Cain is not subduing sin, sin will be subduing him.[7] The problem with Cain is inward; it is his heart. If Cain is not right before

---

[7] In the words of John Owen, "Cease not a day from this work; be killing sin, or it will be killing you." Owen, *The Mortification of Sin* (Glasgow: Christian Focus, 2006), 27.

God, no animal offering can make Cain right. Because of God's warning to Cain in Genesis 4:6-7, apparently sin has been encroaching into Cain's life in subtle and poisonous ways.

We know that Cain is being subdued by wickedness because of the decision he makes regarding his brother. Cain speaks to Abel, and when they are in the field, Cain murders him (Gen 4:8). What words did Cain speak? The text does not tell us. But surely Cain did not share his plan ahead of time with Abel. His words must have been deceptive. And just like sin was ready to pounce on Cain, he pounced on his brother Abel and killed him.

Cain rejected God's warning and chose folly. In a scene reminiscent of Genesis 3, the narrator tells us in Genesis 4 that the Lord asks Cain, "Where is Abel your brother?" (Gen 4:9). This question recalls God's words to Adam, "Where are you?" (Gen 3:9). The difference in the questions is that the Lord asks Cain not about Cain's whereabouts but about *Abel's* whereabouts. The Lord does not ask these questions because he needs information. He asks these questions because the image bearer needs to reckon with what happened. Apart from transparency and confession, repentance will not be genuine.

Though Adam answers the Lord's question truthfully (Gen 3:10, "I heard the sound of you in the garden, and I was afraid, because I was naked, and I hid myself"), Cain rejects the Lord's question and lies: "I do not know; am I my brother's keeper?" (Gen 4:9). He responds to the Lord's question with a question, a statement of arrogance and indifference.

In fact, Cain's question in Genesis 4:9 is the first question from an image bearer in the biblical story line. The question surprises us in its boldness: "Am I my brother's keeper?" The interpreter knows that God is right and Cain is wrong. Cain is supposed to be his brother's keeper. But the way of folly corrupts the way of love. It is no surprise that Cain's wicked heart overflowed in a wicked act against his righteous brother. As an image bearer in God's world, Cain needed to exercise dominion over the sin that crouched and desired to have him. In other words, Cain needed to be wise.

The death of Abel demonstrates a terrible effect of foolishness. Foolishness inhibits a love for neighbor. Cain disobeyed the Lord and harmed his brother, and these actions show that human folly moves in multiple directions, vertically and horizontally. If we are to love God and love neighbor, we need to love wisdom and hate sin. But the narrative of Genesis reports the great love for sin that abounded among the generations.

CALLING UPON THE NAME OF YAHWEH

As Adam's descendants were fruitful and multiplied, the world contained both the wicked and the righteous. In place of Abel, the Lord gave Adam and Eve a son, whom they named Seth (Gen 4:25). And the narrator says that "people began to call upon the name of the Lord" (Gen 4:26). Though Cain and others (like Lamech in Gen 4:23-24) did what was foolish, there were image bearers whose hearts trusted and worshiped the Lord.

The genealogy in Genesis 5 confirms the presence of godly descendants. Enoch, in Genesis 5:21-23, had the unique experience of being "taken" by the Lord apart from earthly death. Enoch's life was one of walking with God (Gen 5:22, 24). The metaphor of walking is about how a person lived. Enoch communed with God and obeyed him. Therefore, his "walk" was wise, and God honored him for it. This honor of being taken was unusual, because the all the surrounding names in the genealogy are lives that ended with a death announcement.

Life in a fallen world was complicated, because the seed of the woman (those who trusted and loved the Lord) lived among the seed of the serpent (those who rebelled against the Lord and took on the spiritual likeness of the evil one). Those who trusted in Yahweh and called upon his name were aware of the hope for a promised son who would defeat the serpent. An example of such hope is clear in the words of Lamech—not the wicked Lamech of Genesis 4:23-24 but the righteous Lamech of Genesis 5:28-31.

Lamech fathered a son and named him Noah, saying, "Out of the ground that the Lord has cursed, this one shall bring us relief from our work and from the painful toil of our hands" (Gen 5:29). Lamech's hope was shaped by the divine promise in Genesis 3:15, that a son from Eve would crush the serpent in victory, a victory that the son would accomplish through his own suffering. Since Lamech's words echoed the hope of Genesis 3:15, that hope would have been more widely known and would have certainly been proclaimed by the first image bearers during the generations after their exile from Eden.

Lamech believed the promise of God, and he hoped for the victorious son. While Noah was not the promised deliverer, Lamech's hope in God was real, and he was among those who called upon the name of the Lord.

FOLLY AND THE FLOOD

According to Genesis 6, wickedness was widespread. The description of the sons of God seeing the daughters of men as "attractive" and then taking any they chose (Gen 6:2) is an intertextual callback to Genesis 3:6, where Eve "saw" that the tree of the knowledge of good and evil was a "delight" to the eyes, and then she "took" of its fruit to eat.

The similarity in the language establishes that sinners are choosing folly outside the garden, generation by generation. There is debate regarding the identities of those participating in the sin of Genesis 6:1-4, but image bearers are certainly involved to some degree. In fact, the Lord's evaluation of the sinful condition is comprehensive and condemning: "The LORD saw that the wickedness of man was great in the earth, and that every intention of the thoughts of his heart was only evil continually" (Gen 6:5). So he pledged to "blot out" humankind from the face of the earth (Gen 6:7).

The great flood was God's judgment on the great folly of humankind. The widespread corruption was clear in the widespread violence (Gen 6:11-12). So God caused water from the ground and from the sky to close like watery jaws on the earth (Gen 7:11-24). Only Noah, his wife, their sons, and their sons' wives survived, and their survival was because of Noah's trust in and submission to God's words. Noah built an ark that endured the flood.

When the waters subsided and the image bearers emerged, God blessed Noah and his sons and said, "Be fruitful and multiply and fill the earth" (Gen 9:1). This commission echoes Genesis 1:28 and confirms that the preflood responsibility continued in Noah's life, as if Noah were a new Adam. Just as Adam and Eve had children of different spiritual conditions, so also did Noah's sons demonstrate the spiritual states of their hearts. Ham's action in Genesis 9:22 brought shame on his father, while Shem and Japheth's actions were wise, discerning, and honoring to their father (Gen 9:23).

Noah's words to Ham were a prophetic judgment. The situation recalls Genesis 3, when shame and nakedness led to consequences (Gen 3:7, 10, 16-19).

Now in Genesis 9 a situation of shame and nakedness leads to judgment. Noah says to Ham, "Cursed be Canaan; a servant of servants shall he be to his brothers" (Gen 9:25). He also speaks regarding his other two sons, "Blessed be the LORD, the God of Shem; and let Canaan be his servant. May God enlarge Japheth, and let him dwell in the tents of Shem, and let Canaan be his servant" (Gen 9:26-27).

The action of Ham, and the corresponding judgment of his offspring (Canaan), confirm that sin and folly did not perish in the flood. Ham had been on the ark, and now his foolishness became known.

A TOWER OF FOOLISHNESS

The opening chapters of Genesis teach us that rebelling against the Lord is foolish, and foolishness reaps judgment. These chapters also teach us that submitting to the Lord's commands is wise, and the wise enjoy the blessing of God. These lessons continue in Genesis 11, in the story of a building project.

In the land of Shinar, people say, "Come, let us make bricks, and burn them thoroughly" (Gen 11:3). The language "Come, let us" is an echo of God's words in Genesis 1. The people in Shinar are image bearers, but the way they speak might suggest a dangerous pursuit. When their plan becomes more explicit, the danger of their thinking becomes clearer to the reader: "Come, let us build ourselves a city and a tower with its top in the heavens, and let us make a name for ourselves, lest we be dispersed over the face of the whole earth" (Gen 11:4).

The desire to "make a name for ourselves" is troubling, because only God's name is worthy of exaltation. Here are image bearers behaving as if they are God. Here are image bearers engaging in a project as if they are going to unite earth to heaven with their tower. The presence of a city probably indicates that the tower was like an ancient ziggurat, a place of worship and theological symbolism.

Human folly makes doctrinal errors. These image bearers in Genesis 11 cannot build a tower to the heavens. They cannot secure a name for themselves when they exist in the image of one who is greater. Because the unity of the people manifests in dishonorable activity, the Lord disperses them. He says,

"Come, let us go down and there confuse their language, so that they may not understand one another's speech" (Gen 11:7).

The confusion of human language impedes their united plans for self-exaltation and false worship. Such confusion results in dispersion. Though they wanted to avoid being dispersed over the face of the earth (Gen 11:4), the outcome is that very thing (Gen 11:9). Human folly in Genesis 11 raised its plans against the Lord, and folly fails. Marks of wisdom include a realization of God's greatness and worth and the importance of honoring him. On the other hand, marks of foolishness include a stubborn delusion of self-aggrandizement and the idea that human plans can prevail over what God has pronounced.

Those builders in Genesis 11:1-9 witnessed the dissolution of their name-building scheme. When we read about God's response to their plans, we learn from the narrator about good and evil. We hear the words of sinners who arrogantly presume with their words ("Come, let us"), and the outcome shows us the failed path of their rebellion.

CONCLUSION

The goal of this chapter is to lay the foundation for the Bible's teaching about wisdom, and this foundation depends on the Bible's first book.[8] The words *wise* and *wisdom* do not appear in Genesis 1–11, but wise and foolish actions appear throughout. Obedience and blessing and life hold together like a threefold cord not easily broken. And disobedience and judgment and death go together as well.

In the Garden of Eden was a tree called the tree of the knowledge of good and evil, and the notion of knowing good and evil is part of the concept of wisdom. Yet, seizing moral autonomy in the hope for more wisdom is not only unwise; it is also detrimental to our lives as image bearers. God has made us to represent him faithfully in his world, that we might subdue and

---

[8] As Belcher puts it, "The God of creation is the God of salvation history. Genesis 1–3 contains all the elements of order, disorder, covenant, law and the beginnings of salvation history. These facts do not prove that Genesis 1–3 is wisdom literature, but it is important that these ideas are closely associated with each other in this foundational text." Richard P. Belcher Jr., *Finding Favour in the Sight of God: A Theology of Wisdom Literature*, New Studies in Biblical Theology (Downers Grove, IL: IVP Academic, 2018), 13.

exercise dominion. But the path of foolishness is marked by crouching sins seeking to devour us, seeking to conquer and subdue us. Human folly rejects God's good design and good commands. The Genesis narratives show the delusion of sinners and the consequences of their defiance.

When we read Genesis 3:15 and Genesis 5:29, we see that our hope is that a promised son will undo the fruit of human folly and overcome the curse of sin and death. If divine wisdom has made the world, divine wisdom can also save the world.

Chapter Two

RIGHTEOUS SUFFERING AND SPIRITUAL WARFARE

BEFORE THE PROMISE TO THE PATRIARCHS about Canaan, before the Sinai covenant in a scene of thunder and power, and before there was a nation that descended from Jacob's sons, there was a man named Job who lived in the land of Uz.

The book that tells Job's story is a long and winding road that goes through agonies and accusations, Satanic opposition and divine confrontation. We meet several friends along the way who prove to be more problematic than helpful. Through it all we can track Job's insistence that his suffering is not due to wickedness against the Lord or others. More than a story about suffering, the book of Job is concerned about wisdom.[1] Job's friends believe they are wise and that Job is foolish, and all of them—including Job—believe wisdom comes from God.

Job's suffering is a catalyst for larger considerations, such as who is thinking rightly about life and the world and God, who understands the origin of

---

[1]For the book of Job's emphasis on wisdom, see Tremper Longman III, *The Fear of the Lord Is Wisdom: A Theological Introduction to Wisdom in Israel* (Grand Rapids, MI: Baker Academic, 2017), chap. 3.

wisdom, and who actually shows himself wise. Not everything Job's friends say is wrong, and not everything Job says is right. Things in this story, as in life, are not so simple.

LISTENING TO THE NARRATOR

According to the first verse of the book, Job lived in the land of Uz, which was an area outside the land of Canaan. Scholars do not agree where exactly Uz was located, though Job is called "the greatest of all the people of the east" (Job 1:3). Perhaps the eastward reference means somewhere east of the Jordan River.

There are challenges to identifying the time Job lived, but a few clues point to an early period in biblical history. First, Job lived a long time (Job 42:16), and such length of life—even longer than Moses' and Joshua's lives—would place him in the kind of lifespans we see before the flood (such as in Gen 5) or possibly after the flood yet before the patriarchs (such as in Gen 11). Second, Job offered sacrifices as the head of his household, and such household altars and offerings were part of an era before or during the patriarchs. Describing the sacrificial practices of the Israelites, the biblical authors highlight the nation's Levitical priesthood and the institution of the tabernacle system and its ceremonial laws. Job, however, is the priest of his own home, offering his own sacrifices—and not at a tabernacle or temple. Third, the book of Job does not contain references to the nation of Israel, formal covenants (like the Abrahamic or Sinaitic or Davidic), events such as the exodus or conquest, or key places such as the city of Jerusalem. Perhaps the absence of these references means that Job's story took place early in biblical history.

The narrator does not tell us everything we'd like to know about Job and his time frame, but we do learn what we need to know. The opening verse of the book says Job "was blameless and upright, one who feared God and turned away from evil" (Job 1:1).[2] This narration matters because the friends of Job are going to challenge his blamelessness. The literary placement of a description of Job's character is significant, then, because the events that follow are not a result of godless behavior or reckless living.

---

[2]Longman says, "In the first few verses, the narrator introduces Job as the epitome of the sage" (*Fear of the Lord*, 43).

Job fears the Lord. The narrator tells us this but also supports it. Job has many sheep, camels, oxen, and donkeys, and many servants (Job 1:3). These truths would suggest to others that he is very blessed. He has a big family as well: seven sons and three daughters—ten children (Job 1:2). In case his children have sinned, Job offers daily sacrifices on their behalf (Job 1:5). Such a practice suggests his love for God and his concern for the spiritual well-being of his family.

The opening line of the book refers to Job as "blameless and upright," which are terms not of his sinlessness but of his devotion and exemplary conduct. The narrator tells us the Lord's own evaluation of Job: "a blameless and upright man, who fears God and turns away from evil" (Job 1:8).

We should believe the narrator's evaluation and not the upcoming accusations about Job's character. The book shows that Job is wise because he fears the Lord, and fearing the Lord is the beginning of wisdom (Prov 9:10). His reverence for God is coupled with a right response to wickedness: he turns from evil.

Because of the book's opening chapter, we can conclude that Job is a righteous man, and the suffering he is going to endure comes *not* as a result of unrighteousness. The narrator has prepared us to see Job as a righteous sufferer.

THINGS UNSEEN AND UNHEARD

The Lord and Satan speak (Job 1:6-7), and the Lord says, "Have you considered my servant Job, that there is none like him on the earth, a blameless and upright man, who fears God and turns away from evil?" (Job 1:8).[3] These are words Job does not hear, and they are part of a scene Job does not see. The importance of recognizing this is that Job's suffering unfolds in a larger context of spiritual warfare.

Satan believes that Job fears the Lord only because the Lord has blessed Job so abundantly (Job 1:9-10). He tells the Lord, "Stretch out your hand and touch all that he has, and he will curse you to your face" (Job 1:11). The reader is left to wonder whether Satan will be proven right. Will Job turn against

---

[3] This being whom the narrator calls Satan is the same figure whom the New Testament calls Satan or "the devil" or "that ancient serpent" (Rev 12:9; see also 2 Cor 11:3, 14). He is the archnemesis of God's people and the lying serpent from Eden's garden (Gen 3:1).

the Lord and curse him? Will Job's hardships undermine his devotion? Satan certainly thinks so.

After the loss of Job's livestock and children, there is another heavenly scene reported by the narrator. The Lord tells the devil about Job, "He still holds fast his integrity, although you incited me against him to destroy him without reason" (Job 2:3). The devil's reply: "Skin for skin! All that a man has he will give for his life. But stretch out your hand and touch his bone and his flesh, and he will curse you to your face" (Job 2:4-5).

The heavenly conversations are unknown to Job. But the spiritual warfare continues to play itself out. Satan "struck Job with loathsome sores from the sole of his foot to the crown of his head" (Job 2:7). Facing the overwhelming emotional agony of the earlier losses (Job 1:13-19), he now experiences hardship in his health (Job 2:7-8).

Job's wife says to him, "Do you still hold fast your integrity? Curse God and die" (Job 2:9). We do not know her name, but we know her wicked advice. Her words sound like those of Satan, who wants Job to curse the Lord and is confident that suffering will lead to it. The spiritual warfare has shown up in the very words of Job's spouse. He replies, "You speak as one of the foolish women would speak. Shall we receive good from God, and shall we not receive evil?" (Job 2:10). The "evil" Job has received is a reference to the tragic familial and bodily trials.

Job identifies his wife with "the foolish women" (Job 2:10). How does her foolishness manifest? She tells Job to turn from God. She mocks him for holding fast to his integrity. She exhorts him to embrace death. Yet in his distress and grief, he rejects her words. He earlier said, "The LORD gave, and the LORD has taken away; blessed be the name of the LORD" (Job 1:21). Now he says, "Shall we receive good from God, and shall we not receive evil?" (Job 2:10).

While Job's wife's words demonstrate her foolishness, Job's words demonstrate his wisdom. He trusts the sovereignty of God, and he knows that God's authority extends over all things in the world—including the suffering of God's image bearers.

Wisdom involves knowing whose words to heed. The first line of Psalm 1 says, "Blessed is the man who walks not in the counsel of the wicked" (Ps 1:1).

In Job's case, he must not walk according to the counsel of his wife. Turning from the Lord would not solve Job's suffering. When Job remains steadfast and speaks of God's sovereignty over the whole experience, the narrator tells us that Job does not sin with his lips or charge God with wrongdoing (Job 1:22; 2:10). If an interpreter says that Job's words are simply unenlightened or unwise, the narrator's evaluation tells us otherwise.

As Job turns to the Lord and blesses the Lord, he demonstrates why his reputation is as a blameless and upright man who fears the Lord.

THE ERROR OF JOB'S FRIENDS

Job's friends get word of his suffering and came to his aid. Eliphaz, Bildad, and Zophar arrive with sympathy and comfort (Job 2:11). They weep for him and tear their robes, sprinkling dust and assuming a posture of sorrow (Job 2:12-13). For seven days and nights they say nothing, for his great suffering weighs on them all (Job 2:13).

But after a week, they begin to speak, and their words accumulate in a cascade of foolishness. Eliphaz says that the innocent do not perish (Job 4:7-9). The outrageousness of this claim must be seen in light of the fact that Job's children *have* perished. Eliphaz declares that those who sow trouble will reap trouble (Job 4:8). Job's trouble, therefore, is a reaping of what he has sown.

Eliphaz's words set a tone, a trajectory, for the many chapters of speeches that follow. Eliphaz, Bildad, and Zophar will be Job's accusers, urging him to realize that his transgressions are the reason for his suffering. Bildad says, "If your children have sinned against him, he has delivered them into the hand of their transgression" (Job 8:4). These words identify Job's dead children as transgressors who received what they deserved. Zophar asks Job, "Should your babble silence men, and when you mock, shall no one shame you?" (Job 11:3). He believes Job's replies constitute babble that mocks the truth of Job's guilt. "Know then," Zophar says, "that God exacts of you less than your guilt deserves" (Job 11:6).

Job does not believe his friends are sharing wisdom. They are caricaturing his situation, and as a result, they are providing unhelpful counsel. He says, "With God are wisdom and might; he has counsel and understanding" (Job 12:13). He wishes he could argue his case with God himself (Job 13:3).

This confidence means that such a court case would lead to Job's vindication. As far as his friends' supposed wisdom, Job says, "Your maxims are proverbs of ashes; your defenses are defenses of clay" (Job 13:12).

Eliphaz, Bildad, and Zophar operate exclusively with a theology of retribution: the sinful experience suffering as divine judgment. They have no category for a righteous sufferer. In their view, suffering and loss are obviously due to prior wickedness. And so Job's insistence about his innocence seems like deflection and denial to them. They consider it their responsibility to convince Job that he has done something wrong that provoked the judgment of God.

Can sinning against the Lord lead to various consequences? Yes. Physical suffering or even death can result from rebellious activity (see Lev 10:1-3; Jn 5:14; Acts 5:5-10; 1 Cor 11:29-30). And since Job's friends do not have a category for righteous suffering, they automatically assume that a person's hardships are an effect from a discernible sinful cause. They need to realize that not all suffering is the result of the afflicted person's decisions.

Consider the example of Abel in Genesis 4. Because the Lord accepted Abel's offering and not Cain's, we can conclude that Abel was a righteous man (Gen 4:4). So Abel's tragic end was not the result of some sin on his part. His death was the result of Cain's sin. Abel was a righteous sufferer. Consider too the example of Joseph.[4] He was sold by his brothers because of their sin. He was accused by Potiphar's wife even though he had been faithful and self-controlled. He was put in prison because of false accusations. Joseph was a righteous sufferer.

Since the narrator in the book of Job has already told us of Job's blamelessness and honorable reputation, we know that his friends are misguided. A purely retributive theology cannot explain all suffering that people experience. The wise realize they cannot discern causation for everything that happens to them and around them.

THE ORIGIN OF WISDOM

Job does not operate with a purely retributive theology, and that is why he does not buckle under the immense pressure his friends apply. He tells them,

---

[4]I will discuss the story of Joseph more in chapter three.

"Far be it from me to say that you are right; till I die I will not put away my integrity from me. I hold fast my righteousness and will not let it go; my heart does not reproach me for any of my days" (Job 27:5-6).

Those words from Job are strong and confident, but we know they are true, for the narrator has given us insight into Job's heart and life. He has wisdom, and he knows where wisdom comes from. In one of his lengthy responses to his friends, he poses the question, "But where shall wisdom be found? And where is the place of understanding?" (Job 28:12). These are not questions he expects his friends to answer. He says, "Man does not know its worth, and it is not found in the land of the living" (Job 28:13). The land of the living refers to this temporal life on earth. According to Job, then, the source of wisdom is not with people.

So where is wisdom from? Job says, "God understands the way to it, and he knows its place" (Job 28:23).[5] God "saw it and declared it; he established it, and searched it out" (Job 28:27). Job's earlier question is being answered. The ultimate source of wisdom is God himself. This truth explains why the fear of the Lord is the beginning of wisdom for God's image bearers. If we reject the source of wisdom, we will not grow wise.

God says, "Behold, the fear of the Lord, that is wisdom, and to turn away from evil is understanding" (Job 28:28). These words of the Lord confirm that the narrator is right about Job, for Job is a man who fears the Lord and turns from evil (Job 1:1). Job has wisdom because he has God, the one who established wisdom and searched it out.

As the book of Job roots wisdom in the knowledge and ways of God himself, we are being prepared for Job 38–41. In these chapters God confronts Job's limited knowledge. Job's wisdom is derivative. It comes from the one whose knowledge has no bounds.

---

[5]According to Bartholomew and O'Dowd, "Proverbs starts with the fear of the Lord as the beginning of wisdom; Job 28 ends with it. In an intriguing way this mirrors Job's development. His sufferings have confronted him unequivocally with the limitations of his understanding, and his journey must be one back to that foundation of wisdom; but he hasn't the slightest idea how to find his way to that place. His return to that starting point, now to know it more deeply, will only be made possible when wisdom comes to him from outside the creation." Craig G. Bartholomew and Ryan P. O'Dowd, *Old Testament Wisdom Literature: A Theological Introduction* (Downers Grove, IL: IVP Academic, 2011), 182-83.

The first words from the Lord to Job in the book are in Job 38:2-3: "Who is this that darkens counsel by words without knowledge? Dress for action like a man; I will question you, and you make it known to me." As the questions unfold, God exposes the limits of Job's knowledge and presence. Job's knowledge has not governed creation from the beginning, but God's has. Longman says, "The purpose of this exercise is to show Job (and those of us who read his story) that he is not in a position to judge God's ways in the world."[6]

Job's response to these questions is an admission of his low estate: "Behold, I am of small account; what shall I answer you? I lay my hand on my mouth. I have spoken once, and I will not answer; twice, but I will proceed no further" (Job 40:4-5). Wisdom involves the recognition that God alone is God. It involves a humble reception of whatever comes from the hand of God, whether comfort or hardship. It also involves the embrace of our human limits in a way that exalts divine knowledge.

Near the end of the book, Job says, "I know that you can do all things, and that no purpose of yours can be thwarted" (Job 42:2). This is Job's response to what God declared in the immediately preceding chapters (Job 38–41). Job's purposes are thwartable, and he cannot do all things. God, however, is different from image bearers.

Biblical wisdom discerns the truth about God and is glad that God alone is God. Part of Satan's snare in Genesis 3 was the temptation to "be like God" (Gen 3:5). Though Job could not penetrate the mysteries of the world, which God alone could decree and govern, Job's friends spoke as if they possessed divine insight into Job's heart. Their unhelpful counsel flowed from their overconfident hearts and their misguided notions about why suffering happens to people.

In the book as a whole, Job is a wise character before the all-wise God. Wisdom dwells with and in God. Job's words are not perfect in all of his speeches, but he does not want to curse God and die. At the end of the story, not only is Job wiser than his friends, but he is also wiser than his earlier self. In Job 42:5-6 he tells the Lord, "I had heard of you by the hearing of the ear, but now my eye sees you; therefore I despise myself, and repent in dust and ashes."

---

[6]Longman, *Fear of the Lord*, 56.

WISDOM FROM THE SPEECHES

We can distill several lessons from the speeches of the book that will help our own lives as Christ's disciples as we humbly walk before the Lord and pursue wisdom.

First, we should avoid speculating about causes for suffering in the lives of others. People around us will be hurting and trying to endure trials. One way we can increase their sorrow is by laying blame at their feet. Knowing that it is possible to make someone's suffering even worse, we should not pretend to know the thoughts of God about the hearts of people.

Second, we should understand the value of sitting with the afflicted and not trying to solve their suffering. Job's friends say many foolish things in their many speeches. But when the narrator first introduces the friends to us, they have arrived to be with Job and to show him sympathy and comfort (Job 2:11). They spend days just sitting with him and not saying a word (Job 2:13). The trouble with them begins when they start to speak!

Third, we should be aware that people who are undergoing great affliction will think and say untrue things. While a perfect track record of thoughts and words would be ideal for image bearers in a fallen world, that ideal succumbs to the reality of the pressures of circumstances and indwelling sins as well as the fact that we lack the knowledge of God. Even Job says, "Let the day perish on which I was born, and the night that said, 'A man is conceived.' Let that day be darkness! May God above not seek it, nor light shine upon it" (Job 3:3-4). According to these words, Job wished he had never been born. Sometimes during periods of great suffering, we might think and say what we might not have otherwise thought or said.

Fourth, we should remember the righteousness of God. The character of God is a comfort to Job in the book, because he knows God will always do what is right—including vindicating his people. The actions of God toward us are never for our ultimate destruction. In the mysterious sovereignty of God, even our sufferings serve purposes we cannot discern. Through all of our trials, the righteousness of God is an unwavering truth. We never have to fear that God has become malicious toward us or that our sufferings are a result of some unrighteous plan of his.

Fifth, we should remind ourselves that God is always worthy of worship. Our circumstances do not increase or decrease the worthiness of God. When Job says, "The LORD gave, and the LORD has taken away; blessed be the name of the LORD" (Job 1:21), he is articulating a conviction that believers should endeavor to cultivate. We must not be those who praise the Lord only when things go our way. Satan was convinced that Job only served the Lord because of the Lord's many blessings in Job's life (Job 1:10-11). Hardship can have the purifying effect of revealing what our heart is most deeply devoted to. And Job declared that the Lord's name should be praised.

Sixth, we should prepare for suffering by trusting the Lord and seeking wisdom before it happens. The narrator tells us what kind of man Job was before the terrible familial and bodily devastation came. Job was blameless and upright, he feared the Lord and turned from evil, and he was concerned for the spiritual state of his children (Job 1:1, 5). Here was a man, then, who walked with God in an attitude of reverence and submission. That pattern of life is good preparation for suffering because Job lived with his heart already oriented toward the Lord. His character and practices formed a kind of spiritual muscle memory. When his wife told him to curse the Lord, he refused. When his friends accused him with their twisted theology, he rejected their words. Job's responses had been rightly honed over a course of life that exalted the Lord and turned from evil.

Seventh, we should keep in mind that our suffering takes place in a context of spiritual warfare. In the book of Job, the righteous sufferer is in the fight of his life. Whether coming from his wife or his friends, accusations and pressures abound against him. We may wrestle with sickness, doubts, and other hardships, but ultimately we contend with spiritual powers and principalities (Eph 6:12). Walking in the fear of the Lord is a fight. Trusting God when everything seems to fall apart is a battle. Blessing the Lord in the valleys of despair is an act of spiritual resistance against satanic opposition and deception.

CONCLUSION

The letter of James is full of wisdom for followers of Christ, and near the end of the letter, the author points us to the life of Job: "Behold, we consider those blessed who remained steadfast. You have heard of the steadfastness of Job, and you have seen the purpose of the Lord, how the Lord is compassionate and merciful" (Jas 5:11).

A wise life is a steadfast life. Job equips us to walk through valleys not because it answers all of our questions about suffering but because it reminds us of our limits and confronts us with the reality of God's sufficiency, supremacy, righteousness, and wisdom. The point in Job, then, is not the *why* but the *who*—and the who is God himself. More than answering his questions and defending himself against accusations, Job needs the Lord. He needs the one who laid the foundations of the earth, feeds sparrows and mountain goats, holds back the storehouses of snow, and can subdue Leviathan.

No one makes it through this world unscathed. If we are going to be wise in the world God has made, we must know the biblical category of the righteous sufferer. When others see our plight and tell us to curse God and die, let us recognize that serpentine hiss for what it is. The Lord gives, and the Lord takes away. But his worthy name is forever to be praised—and the wise know this.

Chapter Three

WALKING THE PATH TOWARD INHERITANCE

IN A WORLD AFFECTED BY SIN AND DEATH, folly appeals to people. This truth is evident at an early age. When you watch children play together, even the best supervision cannot always curb the signs of selfishness and greed and hatefulness. My wife and I are raising four sons, and the deceptiveness and deeds of sin are obvious—and not just in the children's hearts! We are sinners parenting sinners.

We want to see our children walk in the peace and blessing of God. We want them to seek what is good, reject what is evil, and love God with their whole hearts. We want them to be wise, and we want this for them because we love them. How much greater, then, is the love of God for his image bearers. When God orders the world and calls us to walk in wisdom, he does so because he loves us.

Unfortunately, our disordered selves do not always reject the lies and temptations that bring grief and destruction. The path of walking with God is peppered with the deceptions of our ancient serpentine adversary. The path to our inheritance is through many dangers, toils, and snares. Just ask Abraham.

LEARNING TO BELIEVE GOD

Abraham does not come from ancestors who feared the Lord, since his father, Terah, worshiped other gods (Josh 24:2). When God comes to Abraham and calls him to go to a land of promise, this is a call to true and right worship. God tells him, "Go from your country and your kindred and your father's house to the land that I will show you" (Gen 12:1).

The biblical author reports Abraham's obedience. The seventy-five-year-old Mesopotamian man journeys hundreds of miles west to the land of Canaan. God tells him, "I will make of you a great nation, and I will bless you and make your name great, so that you will be a blessing. I will bless those who bless you, and him who dishonors you I will curse, and in you all the families of the earth shall be blessed" (Gen 12:2-3). Going into the Promised Land, then, involves beholding the future place for his descendants.

Though Adam and Eve were exiled from sacred space (Gen 3:22-24), Abraham's offspring will dwell in a set-apart territory. It is not Eden, but readers may take heart that God set apart a place where Abraham's family will be fruitful and multiply. He tells Abraham, "To your offspring I will give this land" (Gen 12:7). The land of Canaan will be the inheritance of Abraham's offspring.

The promise of offspring in a land of promise is staggering, because Abraham and Sarah have no children of their own. Sarah is barren (Gen 11:30). Abraham wonders whether his servant Eliezer will be the heir, but God says, "This man shall not be your heir; your very own son shall be your heir" (Gen 15:4). A grand promise, indeed. Can such a thing be believed?

God told the patriarch to look to the heavens "and number the stars, if you are able to number them" (Gen 15:5). Abraham beholds the heavens and the uncountable stars. "So shall your offspring be," the Lord says (Gen 15:5). Here is the word and promise of the living God, who called Abraham from Ur and who made the very heavens Abraham sees.

Abraham believes God, and God counts his faith as righteousness (Gen 15:6). God spoke, and Abraham's response is, essentially, "I believe what you have said." That is a wise response because it takes God at his word. Faith is trusting what God has said, what God has promised. Faith is our response to God's revelation. Faith is saying to God, "I believe you."

The early narratives of Abraham's life are instructive for us because growing in wisdom involves learning to trust God, to respond rightly to what he has revealed. The outworking of true faith is wisdom, and wisdom marks the words and deeds of the one who follows God.

Learning to believe God certainly comes with challenges. Our flesh can be skeptical and doubtful. Right after the chapter in which we read of God's promise and covenant with Abraham (Gen 15), we read of Abraham and Sarah's half-baked scheme to accomplish what God had said (Gen 16). The way of wisdom requires patience, and both Abraham and Sarah grow impatient. They have a female servant named Hagar, and Sarah says, "Behold now, the LORD has prevented me from bearing children. Go in to my servant; it may be that I shall obtain children by her," and Abraham listens to her (Gen 16:2).

Walking wisely involves listening well, and Abraham does not listen well. The voice of Sarah directs him in an unwise direction, and that is the way he takes.[1] Abraham and Hagar conceive a son named Ishmael (Gen 16), and this outcome brings difficulty to the family. Abraham has already shown questionable judgment in Genesis 12, when he deceived the Egyptian pharaoh about who Sarah was (Gen 12:11-13). But he also showed bravery and fortitude when he amassed 318 trained men to pursue and rescue his nephew Lot (Gen 14:13-16).

The pursuit of wisdom, for Abraham and for us, is not an untainted journey. The ups and downs in Abraham's life can seem discouraging, but we must keep the perspective that our faith is not perfect. We do not see as clearly as we wish or as consistently as we would hope. The object of our faith, however, *is* perfect. The living God is the unshakable rock for Abraham's faith.

God keeps his promise to Abraham. Because of divine power, barren Sarah conceives, and Isaac is born nine months later. Sarah says, "God has made laughter for me; everyone who hears will laugh over me" (Gen 21:6). While laughter can come from disbelief, such as Sarah's earlier response to God's promise (Gen 18:12-15), laughter can also be the result of seeing the

---

[1] The foolishness of Abraham's choice is made clearer when we notice a parallel with Adam. In Gen 3, Adam listens to the voice of his wife and takes the fruit. In Gen 16, Abraham listens to the voice of his wife and takes Hagar. Neither action is wise.

impossible take place. An old, barren woman does not expect to have a child, and no one else expects it either. Since God made it happen for Sarah, laughter can be the happy response to dead hopes bearing fruit by divine power. While learning to believe God, we learn to laugh at the human pronunciations of what God cannot or will not do. Faith believes what God has said, and the outworking of this faith is wisdom that laughs with delight when the impossible comes to pass.

PHARAOH'S CONFIDENCE IN JOSEPH'S WISDOM

"Father Abraham had many sons," so goes the song, and the line is true. The descendants of Abraham are fruitful and multiply. Abraham has Isaac, Isaac has Jacob, and Jacob has twelve sons. Abraham's great-grandson Joseph stands out as a person to whom the biblical author applies language of wisdom.

When we are first introduced to Joseph and his family, he has God-given dreams about his future, and his brothers are jealous both of what these dreams suggest and of the favoritism Joseph receives from their father, Jacob. They plan to kill Joseph. In a turn of events the author reports in Genesis 37, the brothers spare Joseph's life and sell him to people who take him to Egypt (Gen 37:25-28).

Despite the tragic betrayal by his brothers, Joseph is trustworthy and lives with integrity. He serves in the house of a man named Potiphar, and Potiphar's wife seeks to seduce Joseph. He resists her advances (Gen 39:10).[2] One day, after another advance from her and another refusal from him, she accuses him of wrongdoing, and he ends up in prison (Gen 39:11-20).

The story of Joseph, however, is more than a series of human plots against him. The hand of the Lord is with Joseph, and he blesses Joseph the prisoner. Despite the human efforts against Joseph, the Lord causes him to succeed and to gain credibility. Though the word *wisdom* does not appear in Genesis 39, Joseph has clearly conducted himself with wisdom. His discretion and integrity are confirmed by divine blessing and favor (Gen 39:21-23).

---

[2]Joseph's actions embody the wisdom of Prov 5. Solomon speaks about a forbidden woman, an adulteress, when he says, "Why should you be intoxicated, my son, with a forbidden woman and embrace the bosom of an adulteress?" (Prov 5:20). Joseph resists the advances of the immoral woman.

We can imagine a situation where someone would not have exercised self-control in Potiphar's house. And we can imagine a prisoner conducting himself in a manner that put him at odds with his fellow inmates and the guards. The wisdom of Joseph is evident in his exercise of discretion, self-control, and endurance. Though refusing the advances of Potiphar's wife carried no guarantee that things would turn out well for him, Joseph knew what was right and did what was right. While wisdom cannot guarantee a temporal outcome, it can discern that disobedience to God is not going to improve a situation in the long term. God honored Joseph's faithfulness.

In Genesis 40, Joseph interprets the dreams of two prisoners—a baker and a cupbearer—and this ability becomes known to the pharaoh. The Egyptian leader has dreams of his own that he does not understand, so Joseph appears before him (Gen 41:14). The pharaoh is pleased with Joseph's interpretation and explanation. He says, "Since God has shown you all this, there is none so discerning and wise as you are" (Gen 41:39). This recognition uses the terms *discerning* and *wise*, and we can see how Joseph's God-given ability, or skill, stands distinct in the pharaoh's judgment. Earlier the leader's own magicians and "wise men" were unable to interpret the pharaoh's dreams (Gen 41:8). Their worldly cleverness was insufficient. But Joseph's wisdom and skill are not like worldly wisdom. God enables Joseph to discern and understand.

Evidently wiser than the pharaoh's own magicians and courtiers, Joseph is promoted from prisoner to prince: "You shall be over my house, and all my people shall order themselves as you command. Only as regards the throne will I be greater than you" (Gen 41:40).[3] True wisdom brings order, and this is what Joseph brings. Through his discernment and skill, the coming years of famine do not wreak havoc as they might otherwise have done. Not only do the Egyptians benefit from Joseph's wisdom, but his own brothers leave famine-ridden Canaan to get grain from Egypt, and they unknowingly come into Joseph's presence to request it.

A series of events unfold during which Joseph tests his brothers and assesses their character and truthfulness (Gen 42–44). He does not immediately reveal

---

[3] For a biblical-theological study of Joseph, see Samuel Emadi, *From Prisoner to Prince: The Joseph Story in Biblical Theology*, New Studies in Biblical Theology (Downers Grove, IL: IVP Academic, 2022).

his identity. Not until a scene in Genesis 45 does he tell them, "I am your brother, Joseph, whom you sold into Egypt. And now do not be distressed or angry with yourselves because you sold me here, for God sent me before you to preserve life" (Gen 45:4-5). Though Joseph could not have controlled the events that had happened, his wisdom demonstrates his inner trust in God's providence. God meant for good what his brothers had meant for evil (Gen 50:20).

We do not have to be dream interpreters in order to recognize that wisdom exercises dominion over disorder and brings benefit to others. Such skill is ultimately from the Lord, who enables the discernment and understanding of his people. Wisdom also involves prudence—a proper caution and thoughtfulness when making decisions. Joseph's self-control with Potiphar's wife, as well as his posture of forgiveness toward his brothers, shows wisdom in action.

Joseph's wise conduct increased his credibility in the eyes of others. He was faithful in Potiphar's house and, prior to Potiphar's wife's sexual advances and false accusations, found favor in Potiphar's sight (Gen 39:3-6). But even while in prison Joseph found favor in the sight of the keeper of the prison (Gen 39:21-22). Joseph's endurance and godly character did not buckle under these undesirable circumstances. God honored Joseph's faithfulness and elevated him over Egypt.

We cannot control outcomes, and we do not know what the future holds. What we can do is make the next right decision, the next wise move. Wisdom is about playing the long game. It is about making choices out of a heart committed to honoring the Lord and trusting his good providence. Living wisely means doing the right thing at the right time in the right way. Joseph embodied wise living.

TWO WISE MIDWIVES

When wicked actions seem easier and less costly in the short term, acting wisely takes courage. We see courage and wisdom in the defiance of the midwives in Exodus 1. The latest pharaoh in Egypt feels threatened by the growing Israelite population, so he seeks to disrupt their fruitfulness. He wants the midwives to kill any new Hebrew male babies (Ex 1:16).

Wisdom knows how to avoid wicked orders. The pharaoh's instructions are about murdering infants, so the two midwives do not do as he commanded.

What motivates them? Do they not fear the mighty pharaoh? Do they not fear for their own safety?

The midwives have a higher fear. According to the biblical author, "the midwives feared God and did not do as the king of Egypt commanded them, but let the male children live" (Ex 1:17). The midwives fear *God* above all else. And the fear of the Lord is the beginning of wisdom (Prov 9:10). They know they have been tasked with an evil deed, so they know they must not fulfill it. Murdering babies is an abominable practice. No matter how intimidating the pharaoh might be, and no matter how severe the consequences might be, the midwives are driven by a deeper commitment—a commitment to honor and revere the Lord.

These two women not only *know* what is right; they *do* what is right. If they discerned the wrongfulness of the pharaoh's order and yet carried it out anyway, they would have been unwise and sinful. Sometimes foolishness is appealing because it seems easiest at the time, and going along with the pharaoh's edict would certainly not have put the women at odds with his administration. But they know the horror of what he decreed, and they know they are in the precise position to thwart evil.

The courageous wisdom of Shiphrah and Puah shows a fear of God and saved babies. "So God dealt well with the midwives. And the people multiplied and grew very strong. And because the midwives feared God, he gave them families" (Ex 1:20-21). The midwives could not have known for certain what would be the outcome of their actions. But what they received was the blessing and favor of God for their wise handling of an outrageous situation. Even if their defiance had been exposed and they had received a penalty of death, their actions would still have been wise because their hearts feared the Lord above the wicked pharaoh.

Wisdom is not merely a careful calculation of self-preservation. The saving actions of the two midwives were others-focused, and this focus was shaped by a recognition of several factors. They saw the need for the vulnerable and innocent to be spared from murder. They discerned the wrongfulness of the pharaoh's decree. They knew the strategic position they themselves occupied.

Debate remains about whether the midwives' words to the pharaoh were right or wrong. When he asked them why male Hebrew babies continued to be born, they told him, "Because the Hebrew women are not like the Egyptian women, for they are vigorous and give birth before the midwife comes to them" (Ex 1:19). The midwives said nothing about their motive to fear God and defy the pharaoh's wicked order. Their words, then, were deliberately misleading.

Were the midwives right to deceive the Egyptian king? The biblical author seems to affirm, not critique, their strategy. After their misleading words (Ex 1:19), we read, "So God dealt well with the midwives" (Ex 1:20). The midwives engage in a legitimate use of deception. Their words to the king, though deceptive, are commendable. The narrator does not accuse the midwives of sin; in fact, he says they fear the Lord (Ex 1:17, 21). If the narrator says they feared God and that God dealt well with them because of what they did, we should not frame their actions otherwise, nor should we offer any accusation that the narrator does not make and that would undermine the narrator's statement about them.

In the fear of the Lord, the midwives spoke and acted wisely. God blessed them. Others benefited from their courage.

OUT OF EGYPT AND THROUGH THE SEA

The defiance of Pharaoh continues, and God raises up a deliverer. When a Levite mother gives birth to a son, she hides him for three months (Ex 2:2). Then her daughter places the boy in a basket of bulrushes for the daughter of Pharaoh to find beside the bank of the Nile River (Ex 2:3-5). Pharaoh's daughter needs someone to nurse the child, and in the Lord's providence, the child's actual mother is called for such a role (Ex 2:6-9). The Lord blesses this Levite mother's fear of the Lord and her refusal to submit to Pharoah's wicked edict.

When the time comes for the child to be raised in the house of Pharaoh, the biblical author tells us that the child's name is Moses (Ex 2:10). This child grows to become the man who will lead the Israelites out of captivity. At age eighty, Moses will go before Pharaoh and say, on behalf of the Lord, "Let my people go!"

The way out of captivity—whether that captivity is to folly or to Pharaoh—is to follow the Lord wherever he leads. Through a series of plagues on the Egyptian administration and territory, God demonstrates his mighty hand

and compelling power. After a tenth plague—the death of firstborn sons in Egypt—God leads the Israelites out of captivity through his appointed leader, Moses.

According to the biblical author, "The people of Israel journeyed from Rameses to Succoth, about six hundred thousand men on foot, besides women and children. A mixed multitude also went up with them, and very much livestock, both flocks and herds" (Ex 12:37-38). Already positioned east of the Nile River, the land of Goshen is strategically located for a people who need to make a hasty exit eastward.

The Lord leads the Israelites out of Egypt by a pillar of cloud by day and fire by night (Ex 13:21-22). Their path leads to the Red Sea, where God demonstrates his authority and glory over the waters and over the Egyptians. God pulls the waters up into two towering heaps and then dries the ground below, forming a path for the people to walk across (Ex 14:21-22). As the Egyptians pursue the Israelites, they are destroyed under the walls of water that come crashing on them in divine judgment (Ex 14:27-29).

In response to the Lord's great power, "the people feared the LORD, and they believed in the LORD and in his servant Moses" (Ex 14:31). This response is encouraging, especially in contrast to their panic and dread that gripped their hearts when they first came to the Red Sea (Ex 14:11-12). They told Moses, "It would have been better for us to serve the Egyptians than to die in the wilderness" (Ex 14:12). When their panic found words, these words were doubtful of Yahweh as well as wrong about Egypt. Was Egyptian servitude truly better than journeying through hardship in the wilderness? Had Yahweh truly brought them into the wilderness only to kill them there instead of earlier?

Once the Israelites cross the Red Sea and behold Yahweh's power against the Egyptian forces, the Israelites fear the Lord (Ex 14:31). The question, however, is whether this fear of the Lord will continue. They need a reverence for God deeper than their tendencies toward panic and circumstantial dread. They need a trust in his providence and power that can give them perspective when the path before them does not make sense.

Many tests lie in front of these traveling Israelites. In fact, the road from Egypt to the Promised Land is one long road of tests and challenges. The metaphor of a path is common in wisdom contexts, since a person's life is like a road heading either to blessing or destruction. The Israelites, starting in Exodus, are heading toward the land of inheritance, and this path forms the occasion for their own spiritual road as a nation. If they journey toward the Promised Land but fail to trust the Lord along the way, they will be deviating from the path that mattered most—the path of receiving God's promises by faith and submitting to his guidance.

Moses told Pharaoh that the nation of Israel was God's "firstborn son" (Ex 4:22). They were a corporate son whom God delivered from Egypt, and this son needed to grow up and embrace a life obedience and national wisdom. But if this corporate son of God refused to grow wise in the wilderness, they would face judgment for their folly and rebellion. To grow wise, God would be a father to them and teach them the way of wisdom.

A MOUNTAIN OF REVELATION AND VIOLATION

Traveling east and south, the Israelites head toward Mount Sinai. God promises them, "If you will diligently listen to the voice of the LORD your God, and do that which is right in his eyes, and give ear to his commandments and keep all his statutes, I will put none of the diseases on you that I put on the Egyptians, for I am the LORD, your healer" (Ex 15:26).

The Israelites must *listen* and *do*; they must *give ear* and *keep*. Wisdom is not merely hearing. Wisdom is hearing with a readiness to obey. The Lord lays out a myriad of commands while the nation gathers at the base of Mount Sinai, and the wise response is the embrace of and submission to these commands. There is a relationship between wisdom and God's law. God's commands are for the good of his people as he directs them in true worship and holy living. Wisdom, like God's laws, is for our good. Wisdom orients our lives toward God and neighbor in ways that are honorable. While it may be too simplistic to say that God's laws and wisdom are identical, we can certainly affirm that God's laws are an example of wisdom. His laws are wise and direct his people wisely.[4]

---

[4]Longman writes, "Wisdom, at least proverbial wisdom, has overlapping interests and purposes with law. They both encourage certain behaviors and attitudes and discourage or prohibit other attitudes." Tremper Longman III, *The Fear of the Lord Is Wisdom: A Theological Introduction to*

God descends with power and fearsome majesty in Exodus 19, and he proclaims the Ten Commandments to Israel in Exodus 20. These commandments encompass what it looks like to love God and love neighbor. The various exhortations and prohibitions are for Israel's good because they are from Israel's God, and God is good. His holy and faithful character is reflected in the commands the Israelites hear and receive.

The remainder of Exodus 20 and Exodus 21–23 contain applications and extensions of these commandments. Different cases and "if-then" situations help the Israelites think through what living wisely in community will look like. Moses reads this Book of the Covenant to the people, and they agree to obey it (Ex 24:3). Then he sheds an animal's blood, which he throws against the altar and on the Israelites (Ex 24:6-7). Thus God forms a covenant with the Israelites at Sinai (Ex 24:8).

Crucial to Israel's life as God's covenant people is God's law, which directs them in wisdom and away from folly. They are heading toward an occupied land, and Canaan is filled with the folly of false worship and immorality and injustice. For the Israelites to live as God's covenant people in that land, they need to trust the goodness of God's law and conform their lives to its wisdom.

If the Israelites enter the Promised Land and imitate the godlessness of its inhabitants, they will be forsaking the covenant law and thus rejecting the God of the covenant. God tells them, "If you serve their gods, it will surely be a snare to you" (Ex 23:33). One way to identify folly is to identify what ensnares you. False gods are snares because idol worship dishonors God and demeans God's image bearers.

God's commandments direct his people toward what is good and away from what corrupts and destroys. The Israelites learn this lesson the hard way when Moses descends the mountain with revelation from the Lord in

---

Wisdom in Israel (Grand Rapids, MI: Baker Academic, 2017), 170. One difference between biblical wisdom and laws is that proverbial wisdom is not universally true; it is appropriate at the right time and in the right manner (see, e.g., Prov 26:4-5, which teach that sometimes we should correct and teach a fool, while other times we should not correct and teach a fool). God's laws, such as the Ten Commandments, however, are binding. Wisdom and laws, Longman says, "are closely related—maybe not siblings, but close cousins. . . . Law and wisdom are closely tied in yet another way. Obeying the law and living according to wisdom leads to reward, and disobedience to law leads to punishment" (172).

Exodus 32. While Moses was on Mount Sinai, the Israelites were at the base of the mountain building a golden calf (Ex 32:1-6). They rejected God's commands and made an idol to worship. Their pursuit of folly leads to judgment, and thousands of Israelites die (Ex 32:27-29, 35).

The judgment at Sinai is a visual demonstration of where folly leads. If the Israelites are to walk the road from Sinai to Canaan, they need to walk an inner path of wisdom and submission. Apart from submission to God's commands, sin will be their undoing. God tells them, "Take care, lest you make a covenant with the inhabitants of the land to which you go, lest it become a snare in your midst" (Ex 34:12). When the Israelites enter the land, they will show whether they truly believe God's warnings. In fact, troubling things will be revealed not long after leaving Sinai.

A GENERATION FULL OF FOLLY

When we read about false worshipers dying in Exodus 32, we hope that Israel's ranks have been purged of covenant breakers. But as the Israelites depart from Mount Sinai in Numbers 10, there are signs of trouble on the horizon. In Numbers 11 the people complain in the hearing of the Lord (Num 11:1), and later, in their strong cravings, they express fond remembrance of the menu back in Egypt (Num 11:4-6).

Wisdom does not distort the truth, and it rightly discerns the deception of sin. The Israelites in Numbers 11 do not show discernment. They caricature their life in Egypt with alluring language (Num 11:4-5), and they speak with condescension about the daily miracle of manna that God has given to them: "But now our strength is dried up, and there is nothing at all but this manna to look at" (Num 11:6). A wise response from the people would have been to believe God's promises and to receive daily sustenance with gratitude.

Murmurs and resistance come to a head in Numbers 13–14, when the exodus generation is willing to reject the land of promise. Coming near the land, Moses sends twelve spies into Canaan to return with a report about the produce and the people. Forty days pass, and the spies return with a negative report: "The people who dwell in the land are strong, and the cities are fortified and very large. And besides, we saw the descendants of Anak there" (Num 13:28). Though Caleb calls for the people to go up and occupy the land at once, the others resist Caleb's exhortation. They say, "We are not able to go up against the people, for they are stronger than we are" (Num 13:31).

This bad report discourages and grieves the people. The Israelites weep and grumble, eventually expressing their wish to have died in the land of Egypt or in the wilderness (Num 14:1-2). The words of the Israelites are utter foolishness. They are ready to reject the Promised Land because they are afraid the inhabitants will kill them, even though God promised the land would be for his people. Their foolishness stems from their fear and from their disbelief in God's promises.

The Lord says, "How long will this people despise me? And how long will they not believe in me, in spite of all the signs that I have done among them?" (Num 14:11). Human folly leads to despising the Lord. Human folly ignores obvious reasons for trusting the Lord. The Israelites exhibit this folly when they are ready to choose a new leader and return to Egypt (Num 14:4). Their foolish eyes see their former condition in slavery as more desirable than walking by faith into the Promised Land. Though God said he would overcome his enemies, the Israelites believe their worldly assessment of the situation. The enemies seem too many and too strong.

In response to the rebellion that spreads throughout this older generation of Israelites, God proclaims a forty-year judgment. For forty years these Israelites will wander in the wilderness until the last of this exodus generation dies (Num 14:29, 33-34). The grumbling and rebellion of the Israelites reap hardship and divine displeasure. Faithlessness does not reap blessing.

As a generation of foolish Israelites dies in the wilderness, a new generation grows up to enter the land under Joshua's leadership. Until that time when Joshua crosses the Jordan with the Israelites, Moses shepherds the stiff-necked people who will die before inheriting the land. Their inheritance is the wilderness. The place of their rebellion becomes their graves.

LOVING AND FEARING THE LORD

In order to prepare the new generation of Israelites to receive and conquer the land of promise, Moses gives a series of speeches—found in the book of Deuteronomy—that both remind and exhort the people about crucial things.

A substantial portion of the opening chapters of Deuteronomy is a recounting of Israel's recent history, a recounting that includes the unsavory truth of their ancestors' rebellion and judgment. Moses intends for his sermons to orient the people through retelling their history and reiterating divine commands.

After reviewing the Ten Commandments (Deut 5:6-21; see Ex 20:1-17), Moses tells the new generation of Israelites, "You shall love the Lord your God with all your heart and with all your soul and with all your might" (Deut 6:5). Fifteen hundred years later, Jesus will call those words the greatest commandment (Mt 22:37-38).

The "love" command in Deuteronomy 6:5 is all-encompassing because the language refers to a person's heart, soul, and might. With all that the Israelites are, they are to love God. This responsibility is not just theirs. It is ours as well, because God was worthy then and is worthy now. With all that we are, we are to love the Lord.

How will such love manifest in the lives of the Israelites? In the next verse, Moses says, "And these words that I command you today shall be on your heart" (Deut 6:6). The most obvious connection between Deuteronomy 6:5 and Deuteronomy 6:6 is the "heart" language. The Israelites are to love God with their heart, and God's words are to be on their heart. These notions are inseparable because we all live out what is in our hearts. For the Israelites to love God with their hearts, they need hearts shaped by the words of God.

Without a knowledge of what God has said, how can they properly love him? How can they have a fear of the Lord? How can they live wisely? This new generation not only needs to hold to God's words; they need to teach these commands to their children so that a future generation of Israelites will grow up with a knowledge of the living God. The Promised Land is to be a place of widespread worship of Yahweh, not a place of idolatry and rebellion (Deut 6:10-12).

Though the Canaanites worship other gods, the Israelites are to devote themselves to the true worship of the one true God. Moses says, "It is the Lord your God you shall fear. Him you shall serve and by his name you shall swear. You shall not go after other gods, the gods of the peoples who are around you" (Deut 6:13-14). False worship compromises true love for God and a true fear of God.

Fearing God and loving God are related notions. While not necessarily equivalent, they seem to be logically connected in this way: those who love God will fear him, and those who do not love him will not fear him. We might even say that fearing God is a way in which love for God bears fruit. If you love God with your heart and soul and might (Deut 6:5), you will fear the Lord (Deut 6:13).

Reverence for God is the result of a heart rightly ordered to God in truth. A rightly ordered heart will mean a life wholly devoted to God. The words *heart* and *soul* and *might* (Deut 6:5) constitute our allegiance. Whatever our heart, soul, and might are most devoted to, that object—whether God or something other than God—has our allegiance. According to Moses' command in Deuteronomy 6:5, our ultimate allegiance should be to our Creator and Redeemer. The first of the Ten Commandments, after all, says, "You shall have no other gods before me" (Deut 5:7).

If we love God with our heart, that love will show up in our life. We will fear, or honor, the Lord. One way to define "the fear of the Lord" is living out a love for God in all of life.

Each part of that definition matters. The phrase "living out" emphasizes the obedient response in one's life to what God has said. Following God is not merely an internal disposition, though the disposition certainly matters. True "love for God" will not remain unknown. Love for God is lived out. And what is the scope of this "lived out" love for God? Your whole life is the scope. God's commands leave no realm of our lives unaddressed.

Because we live out what we most deeply love, and because we demonstrate where our allegiance lies in light of how we direct our heart and soul and might, the state of our heart is critical to the Bible's commands. Moses reminds the Israelites that the wilderness tests revealed the hearts of their ancestors: "And you shall remember the whole way that the Lord your God has led you these forty years in the wilderness, that he might humble you, testing you to know what was in your heart, whether you would keep his commandments or not" (Deut 8:2).

The pressures of circumstances in the wilderness served to test the Israelites and to reveal what was in their hearts. This new generation needs this reminder so that they can ponder their own hearts and the object of their allegiance. Moses says, "So you shall keep the commandments of the Lord your God by walking in his ways and by fearing him" (Deut 8:6). If they do not obey him, they do not fear him. If they do not obey him, they do not love him. If they do not keep his commandments, they are not walking in his ways.

Near the end of Deuteronomy, Moses speaks to the Israelites in a way that showcases the two paths before them: "See, I have set before you today life and good, death and evil" (Deut 30:15). Furthermore, "I call heaven and earth to witness against you today, that I have set before you life and death, blessing and curse. Therefore choose life, that you and your offspring may live, loving the Lord your God, obeying his voice and holding fast to him" (Deut 30:19-20).

Moses sets before them life and death, good and evil, wisdom and folly. If the Israelites walk in wisdom, their lives will not be hidden in a corner. The surrounding peoples will see them, like seeing light shining in the darkness. Moses says,

> See, I have taught you statutes and rules, as the Lord my God commanded me, that you should do them in the land that you are entering to take possession of it. Keep them and do them, for that will be your wisdom and your understanding in the sight of the peoples, who, when they hear all these statutes, will say, "Surely this great nation is a wise and understanding people." (Deut 4:5-6)

When Jesus tells his disciples, "If you love me, you will keep my commandments" (Jn 14:15), his words sound like the kind of thing God would say to his people in the Old Testament. If there is no love for God, there is no fear of God. And if there is no fear of God, there is no life of wisdom, because the fear of the Lord is the beginning of wisdom (Prov 9:10).

CONCLUSION

The stories of Abraham and his descendants show the reality of snares that test one's allegiance and reveal the heart. Following God involves learning to believe what he has said and to walk in light of it. God calls his people to honor him and obey him, and this obedience is not mere outward conformity. We need an inner disposition, a love for God that starts inward but does not remain inward. We need to fear the Lord. We need to live out a love for God in all of life.

Like the Israelites, we face the temptation to believe worldly fears and to be suspicious of God's commands and wisdom. We are not immune to snares. To bolster our confidence in God's goodness and ways, we need to study the folly of the wilderness generation. Too often the path toward the Promised Land was marked by disbelieving and rebellious voices. What does our speech sound like? What do life's circumstances and hardships reveal about our hearts through our words?

We are called to worship him whose mighty hand and outstretched arm delivered the Israelites out of Egypt and through walls of water. This same God of wonders spoke wisdom from Sinai and sustained the wilderness wanderers. Through dangers, toils, and snares, the people of God must learn to trust the Lord, for they are sons and daughters guided by a loving Father who has their best interest at heart.

Chapter Four

WHAT WAS RIGHT IN THEIR OWN EYES

SOMETIMES A FICTION WRITER sets books in the same universe, with characters and events and themes that overlap and build as the books develop. Think of the Narnia stories or the Middle-earth tales. What C. S. Lewis and J. R. R. Tolkien are doing is something that is not accomplished in one book. Rather, a series of books tells the big story, and the later books rely on knowledge from earlier ones. The Bible works this way.

The biblical authors are telling the True Story of the world, and the deeper we get into the Old Testament literature, the more its earlier knowledge and events will be assumed and echoed in these later books. When we read the books of Joshua and Judges, for instance, we should do so in light of the Torah—the five books of Moses that are the foundational texts for everything that follows.

The narratives in Joshua and Judges continue to demonstrate that the Israelites were supposed to live wisely in the Promised Land, yet they were a compromised people. The inhabitants and idols of the land became a snare to them—just as God said they would.

THE NOTION OF DRIFT

God told the Israelites to avoid the snares of idolatry, but this avoidance would require obedience on their part—a *deliberate pursuit* of the living God through true worship. Wisdom is not the kind of thing you drift into. The reason for this is that the world is not a neutral space, and the human heart is not a neutral place. Left to ourselves and the operations of indwelling sin, we do not naturally drift toward holiness and wisdom. This world's current is strong and carries us away from the noble path.

Since the world and our hearts are not neutral, wisdom must be the deliberate pursuit of our lives. Do not expect to simply grow wise as you age. Have you not met foolish older people? Have you not met adults who never seemed to grow up and who conduct themselves in morally abominable ways? Getting older will not necessarily mean getting wiser.

The new generation of Israelites had been growing up during the forty-year wilderness period, but they would be remiss to assume that their survival of the wilderness would lead to a prosperous future in the Promised Land. If they did not pursue wisdom, foolishness would destroy them. If they did not walk a different moral path from their forebears, they would reap the judgment of the Lord and be exiled from the land of their inheritance.

Who would lead them into their inheritance and, along the way, lead by example as well? Moses' own life loomed large over the Pentateuch, so his death left a deep vacancy in the nation's leadership. The biblical author says, "And there has not arisen a prophet since in Israel like Moses, whom the Lord knew face to face, none like him for all the signs and wonders that the Lord sent him to do in the land of Egypt, to Pharaoh and to all his servants and to all his land, and for all the mighty power and all the great deeds of terror that Moses did in the sight of all Israel" (Deut 34:10-12).

Right before those final verses in Deuteronomy—and the Pentateuch—we see good news about Joshua: "And Joshua the son of Nun was full of the spirit of wisdom, for Moses had laid his hands on him. So the people of Israel obeyed him and did as the Lord had commanded Moses" (Deut 34:9).

The spirit of wisdom indwells Joshua, which means that his heart and life are rightly ordered by the Word of God. The Lord tells Joshua, "This Book of the Law shall not depart from your mouth, but you shall meditate on it day and night, so that you may be careful to do according to all that is written in it. For then you will make your way prosperous, and then you will have good success" (Josh 1:8).

For Joshua to lead wisely and to walk a prosperous path, he needs to adhere to—and not depart from—God's Word. If Joshua and the Israelites are devoted to God's commands, they will not drift into the folly of idolatry. The people express their willingness to follow Joshua: "All that you have commanded us we will do, and wherever you send us we will go. Just as we obeyed Moses in all things, so we will obey you. Only may the LORD your God be with you, as he was with Moses!" (Josh 1:16-17).

JOSHUA'S PERSONAL CONCERNS

As the new Moses, Joshua leads the Israelites over the Jordan River and begins the conquest of the Promised Land. The biblical author records the victories in southern and northern Canaan, as well as the many defeated kings (Josh 10–12). Many years later, when Joshua is an old man and nearing death, he gives a charge to Israel's leaders. His words echo the kind of emphasis in the Lord's charge to him before the conquest.

Joshua says,

> Therefore, be very strong to keep and to do all that is written in the Book of the Law of Moses, turning aside from it neither to the right hand nor to the left, that you may not mix with these nations remaining among you or make mention of the names of their gods or swear by them or serve them or bow down to them, but you shall cling to the LORD your God just as you have done to this day. (Josh 23:6-8)

Verses later, Joshua tells them, "Be very careful, therefore, to love the LORD your God" (Josh 23:11).

In Joshua 23, we see two teachings working together: the call to carefully keep God's commands and the call to carefully love the Lord. The obedience of the Israelites is how their love for Yahweh will manifest. If they refuse his law and disregard his revelation, can they in the same breath claim to love the Lord? Their claim would be meaningless.

To motivate their love for God and their confidence in God's good commands, the Israelites need to remember "that not one word has failed of all the good things that the Lord your God promised concerning you. All have come to pass for you; not one of them has failed" (Josh 23:14). God has established sufficient credibility with his covenant people. They have no reason *not* to trust him, and they have every reason *to* trust him. If God's promises are utterly trustworthy, then the Israelites should weigh his warnings with the same confidence.

Joshua warns them, "But just as all the good things that the Lord your God promised concerning you have been fulfilled for you, so the Lord will bring upon you all the evil things, until he has destroyed you from off this good land that the Lord your God has given you" (Josh 23:15). A future of flourishing is connected to their submission to God's commands. In places such as Leviticus 26 and Deuteronomy 28, God promised covenant curses on the covenant people if they rejected his law and instead pursued the gods and ways of the nations. If the Israelites sow foolishness, they will reap destruction. If they live wisely, they will flourish under God's blessing.

In the final chapter of the book that bears his name, Joshua says, "Now therefore fear the Lord and serve him in sincerity and in faithfulness. Put away the gods that your fathers served beyond the River and in Egypt, and serve the Lord" (Josh 24:14). A proper fear of Yahweh is connected to a sincere heart. A sincere heart is the opposite of a divided or hypocritical heart. Fearing Yahweh is a not a posture void of substance. Fearing Yahweh is an attitude of reverence, and it is demonstrated in obedience to his commands. If they say, "We fear God," yet walk in ways of darkness, they will be false in their words and deluded in their hearts.

The gathered Israelites hear Joshua's exhortations and respond, "Far be it from us that we should forsake the Lord to serve other gods" (Josh 24:16). They insist, "Therefore we also will serve the Lord, for he is our God" (Josh 24:18). According to their words, then, they are ready to receive Joshua's exhortations into their hearts and lives. They are ready to submit to God's commands and reject the ways of idolatry.

But Joshua is not as sure of them as they are. He responds to their response, "You are not able to serve the Lord, for he is a holy God. He is a jealous God;

he will not forgive your transgressions or your sins. If you forsake the Lord and serve foreign gods, then he will turn and do you harm and consume you, after having done you good" (Josh 24:19-20).

At first his words seem discouraging. He is skeptical of their zealous verbal commitment. Yet when we consider Joshua's experience with the Israelites, he knows of Moses' difficulties with their ancestors, and he knows that this new generation is not blameless. During the rest of Joshua's years, the Israelites serve the Lord (Josh 24:31).

But things changed when a subsequent generation of Israelites grows up. After the conquest generation dies, "there arose another generation after them who did not know the Lord or the work that he had done for Israel" (Judg 2:10).

EVIL IN THE SIGHT OF THE LORD

If the generation that arose after Joshua's death does not know the Lord or what the Lord has done, that ignorance suggests the prior generation's failure to proclaim his identity and deeds to the next. According to Judges 2:11-12, "the people of Israel did what was evil in the sight of the Lord and served the Baals. And they abandoned the Lord, the God of their fathers, who had brought them out of the land of Egypt. They went after other gods, from among the gods of the peoples who were around them, and bowed down to them. And they provoked the Lord to anger."

Foolishness does not prioritize what matters in the eyes of the Lord. Foolishness is doing things your own way without regard for the Lord or what he has said. The narratives in the book of Judges teach us about wisdom and folly because they tell of Israel's rebellion and the subsequent distresses that come their way.

Rejecting the Lord brings grief:

> The anger of the Lord was kindled against Israel, and he gave them over to plunderers, who plundered them. And he sold them into the hand of their surrounding enemies, so that they could no longer withstand their enemies. Whenever they marched out, the hand of the Lord was against them for harm, as the Lord had warned, and as the Lord had sworn to them. And they were in terrible distress. (Judg 2:14-15)

If you substitute idols for the worship of the living God, you are acting as his enemy. And if you want the same gods as his enemies, you will receive the same treatment as his enemies. The Lord's hand is against the rebel Israelites. They should not expect that things will go well for them on the path of folly. Biblical narratives such as those found in Judges show us where folly leads.

The snares of idolatry remain because the conquest of Canaan is incomplete. Due to Israel's transgressions, the Lord will no longer drive out the nations (Judg 2:23). Instead, the pagan inhabitants will be a means of revealing what is in the covenant people's hearts: "They were for the testing of Israel, to know whether Israel would obey the commandments of the Lord, which he commanded their fathers by the hand of Moses" (Judg 3:4). This language in Judges 3:4 is similar to Deuteronomy 8:2, where Moses spoke of the forty-year wilderness journey as when God was "testing you to know what was in your heart, whether you would keep his commandments or not."

Tests in the wilderness revealed the kind of people who were traveling through it, and tests in Canaan reveal the kind of people who are occupying it. At some point and in some way, the state of Israel's national heart will be made clear. According to Judges 3:7, "They forgot the Lord their God and served the Baals and the Asheroth." If the Israelites have forgotten the Lord—meaning, they have turned from his commandments and gone after idols—then not only will their own covenant standing be in jeopardy, but they will also display corrupt worship among the nations. And if the nations need to witness true worship and see God-honoring obedience, then wayward Israelites will not be a light to these nations. While wisdom shines light, folly joins the darkness.

Moses was speaking about God's commands when he said,

> Keep them and do them, for that will be your wisdom and your understanding in the sight of the peoples, who, when they hear all these statutes, will say, "Surely this great nation is a wise and understanding people." For what great nation is there that has a god so near to it as the Lord our God is to us, whenever we call upon him? And what great nation is there, that has statutes and rules so righteous as all this law that I set before you today? (Deut 4:6-8)

Obedience to Yahweh will demonstrate wisdom because it will mean the embrace of his commands—and his commands are wise. But what will the nations say if the Israelites do not keep these commands? They cannot rightly consider Israel a wise and understanding people. The Israelites need to dwell in the Promised Land with an abiding sense of the greatness (and nearness) of Yahweh as well as the righteousness and goodness of his law.[1]

But from the book of Judges we learn that the covenant people did not do what was right in God's sight. Multiple times, near the end of the book, there is a refrain:

> In those days there was no king in Israel. Everyone did what was right in his own eyes. (Judg 17:6)
>
> In those days there was no king in Israel. (Judg 18:1)
>
> In those days, when there was no king in Israel . . . (Judg 19:1)
>
> In those days there was no king in Israel. Everyone did what was right in his own eyes. (Judg 21:25)

Four times we are told there was no king in Israel. In the opening and ending occurrences of that report, another claim is made: everyone did what was right in his own eyes. We would be hard-pressed to find a better definition in the Bible for folly. As people do what seems right to them, they are working out of a heart that has been corrupted by sin. As people do what seems right to them, the standard they are living by is subjective rather than objective. We could even apply this language to Eve's sin in Genesis 3. According to the biblical author, "when the woman saw that the tree was good for food, and that it was a delight to the eyes, and that the tree was to be desired to make one wise, she took of its fruit and ate" (Gen 3:6).

Eve did what was right in her own eyes. Adam did the same, for he took the fruit from her and ate it also (Gen 3:6). When the book of Judges tells us

---

[1] According to Bartholomew and O'Dowd, "The instruction (Torah) provided by law is inseparably related to creation order and thus provides the Israelites with wisdom and discernment. God's creation by wisdom is foundational to all that follows in the drama of Scripture so that one can see how all the streams of Old Testament literature—narrative, law, prophecy, psalms—are designed to enable the Israelites to live wisely as God's people." Craig G. Bartholomew and Ryan P. O'Dowd, *Old Testament Wisdom Literature: A Theological Introduction* (Downers Grove, IL: IVP Academic, 2011), 294.

that everyone did what was right in their own eyes, it expresses that the Israelites were like the sinning couple in Eden all over again. They were acting in accordance with their personal desires without regard for what God had said.

Doing what is right in your own eyes is evil in God's eyes.[2]

THE NEED FOR A WISE KING

The refrain near the end of Judges, that "there was no king in Israel," creates anticipation for a king. The author is not merely making an observation; he is identifying a problem. Israel needs a leader to unite the nation.[3]

Moses was the leader of the Israelites from Exodus through Deuteronomy, and Moses' successor was Joshua. But Joshua's death (in Josh 24) left a void. Who is the new Joshua? The book of Judges does not report a single replacement for Joshua. No leader rises to assemble the people under new leadership.

What the people need is a wise king who can lead them by both word and example. The Lord told Abraham, "I will make you exceedingly fruitful, and I will make you into nations, and kings shall come from you" (Gen 17:6). So the expectation of a future king was found in God's promises to this patriarch. In Genesis 49, when Jacob was blessing his sons, he said, "The scepter shall not depart from Judah, nor the ruler's staff from between his feet, until tribute comes to him; and to him shall be the obedience of the peoples" (Gen 49:10). Not only should Israel expect a king from Abraham's descendants, but this king will also be from Judah's tribe.

Near the end of the Pentateuch, Moses gave instructions regarding Israel's future kings. The king "must not acquire many horses for himself or cause

---

[2]The teaching in Judg 17:6; 18:1; 19:1; 21:25 emphasizes what is morally wrong. The biblical author indicts the people for doing what was right in their own eyes, because their actions violated God's commands and his covenant stipulations. When we read about people such as the Egyptian midwives who did what seemed right to them (in Ex 1:15-21), their actions are commended by the biblical author because they aligned with and did not contradict God's righteousness. Those who are indicted by the author of Judges, however, had deviated from God's law. What seemed right to them contradicted God's righteousness.

[3]Stephen Dempster writes, "Israel is in need of lasting kingship instead of a temporary judge." Dempster, *Dominion and Dynasty: A Theology of the Hebrew Bible* (Downers Grove, IL: InterVarsity Press, 2003), 133.

the people to return to Egypt in order to acquire many horses, since the Lord has said to you, 'You shall never return that way again.' And he shall not acquire many wives for himself, lest his heart turn away, nor shall he acquire for himself excessive silver and gold" (Deut 17:16-17).

These instructions are about the object of the king's confidence and hope. Israel's king should hope in the Lord, not in many horses—which would denote a vast army. Israel's king should trust in the Lord, not in a vast harem of many wives. Israel's king should be confident in the Lord's power, not in worldly wealth such as silver and gold. The temptation will be for Israel's king to operate like other ancient Near Eastern rulers. But this king is to be different—set apart and devoted to Yahweh above all.

Moses continued talking about the king:

> And when he sits on the throne of his kingdom, he shall write for himself in a book a copy of this law, approved by the Levitical priests. And it shall be with him, and he shall read in it all the days of his life, that he may learn to fear the Lord his God by keeping all the words of this law and these statutes, and doing them, that his heart may not be lifted up above his brothers, and that he may not turn aside from the commandment, either to the right hand or to the left, so that he may commit long in his kingdom, he and his children, in Israel. (Deut 17:18-20)

The king's devotional life is to be immersed in the Torah, and this Torah is to be a copy he himself has diligently made—a copy approved by the priests themselves. The reason the king will avoid false sources of security (in Deut 17:16-17) is that his heart will be shaped and influenced by the Word of God (Deut 17:18-20).

According to Moses, the king "may learn to fear the Lord his God by keeping all the words of this law and these statutes" (Deut 17:19). The fear of the Lord is the beginning of wisdom (Prov 9:10), so the goal of the king's immersion in Scripture is to be a wise king for the people. By not turning aside from God's commands, the king will be leading the people in faithfulness. By setting an example of devotion, the people will have a Torah-knowing and command-delighting ruler who is not swayed by worldly appearances and allurements.

While the Israelites learned from Moses what a future king should be like, the book of Judges tells us there was no king in Israel. The result of no leader to consolidate the people in righteousness was the people's pursuit of their personal desires. They did what seemed right to them. Because of the effects of sin on our minds and hearts, our desires are not the most reliable guide for our words and conduct. If "everyone did what was right in his own eyes," then the Israelites were not operating according to the objective standard of God's law.

A FOOL AS THE FIRST KING

If the Israelites were doing what seemed right to them, then their eventual desire for a king would be inevitably affected by their disordered hearts. Bible readers should not be surprised, then, about the character and leadership of their first king.

When you hear the name Saul, you might think of Saul of Tarsus, also named Paul, who ministered as an apostle of the Lord Jesus for several decades in the first century AD. Saul was from the tribe of Benjamin, and he eventually died a martyr under Emperor Nero in the mid-60s AD. But this Saul was named after an *earlier* Saul—the first king of Israel. While the Saul of the New Testament ended up being a servant of Christ and a proponent of the gospel, the Old Testament Saul ended up being a scourge on the Israelites and an unfit king.

According to 1 Samuel 8, Israelite elders come to the prophet Samuel and say, "Behold, you are old and your sons do not walk in your ways. Now appoint for us a king to judge us like all the nations" (1 Sam 8:5). The monarchy has not been established before that request, yet Samuel discerns problems beneath their words. The Lord tells Samuel, "Obey the voice of the people in all that they say to you, for they have not rejected you, but they have rejected me from being king over them" (1 Sam 8:7).

The problem for the Israelites is not the request for a king but the *kind* of king they want. They insist, "There shall be a king over us, that we also may be like all the nations, and that our king may judge us and go out before us and fight our battles" (1 Sam 8:19-20). The Israelites want to have a king like the nations, and this desire is understood by the Lord and Samuel to be unsound. Their request displeases Samuel (1 Sam 8:6), and it means they are rejecting God's kingship (1 Sam 8:7). The Lord says the people will receive a king "whom you have chosen for yourselves" (1 Sam 8:18). As the people express their desire for a king like the nations, they do not apply the criteria of Deuteronomy 17, criteria a ruler is to meet. In 1 Samuel 8 the Lord tells the prophet to "obey the voice of the people in all that they say to you" (1 Sam 8:7). This king, in other words, will be the result of the people's voice and not the Lord's voice. Even when Samuel warns them about the kind of king they will receive (1 Sam 8:10-18), "the people refused to obey the voice of Samuel" (1 Sam 8:19).

Evidently the Israelites continue to do what seems right in their own eyes, and this includes a demand for a certain kind of ruler—the kind of ruler that signals their rejection of God's kingship over them. The displeasure of God is evident in the king's tribe: Saul is from Benjamin, though the appointed royal tribe is Judah (see Gen 49:10; 1 Sam 9:1-2). So Israel's first king does not even descend from the right tribe.

In an address to the Israelites, Samuel says,

> If you will fear the LORD and serve him and obey his voice and not rebel against the commandment of the LORD, and if both you and the king who reigns over you will follow the LORD your God, it will be well. But if you will not obey the voice of the LORD, but rebel against the command of the LORD, then the hand of the LORD will be against you and your king. (1 Sam 12:14-15)

Samuel's words reveal his concern: the people's rebellion against the Lord. Their response to Samuel might surprise the reader: "Pray for your servants to the LORD your God, that we may not die, for we have added to all our sins this evil, to ask for ourselves a king" (1 Sam 12:19). Hearing this acknowledgment from the people, Samuel tells them to serve the Lord with all their heart and not to turn aside to idols (1 Sam 12:20-21). He wants the people to fear the Lord (1 Sam 12:24). If they refuse to fear the Lord and instead act foolishly, they and their king will face God's judgment (1 Sam 12:25).

King Saul reigns in Israel for forty years (Acts 13:21). And during these decades he commits unlawful deeds. He violates sacrificial procedure (1 Sam 13:8-10), after which Samuel tells him, "You have done foolishly"

(1 Sam 13:13). He makes a rash vow, which leads his son to say, "My father has troubled the land" (1 Sam 14:29). He does not obey the Lord by defeating the Amalekites (1 Sam 15:18-19). He tries to kill David (1 Sam 19:1). He executes priests of the Lord (1 Sam 22:21). He consults a medium at En-dor (1 Sam 28:7-8).

The first king of Israel was a fool. Saul did not keep God's commands, he did not lead the Israelites in righteousness, and he did not fear the Lord.

CONCLUSION

Reporting Israel's history after the exodus but before the monarchy, the biblical authors narrate their departure from Yahweh's commands. Though Moses and Joshua were faithful leaders, the period of the judges was characterized by rebellion. If the Israelites were to keep God's law and live as light among the Canaanites, God would bless them and defend them and dwell with them. But if they compromised their national mission and imitated the false worship of the Canaanites, the Israelites would fall under divine judgment.

What Israel needed was a king, lest everyone continue doing what was right in their own eyes. But when the people desired a king to rule over them, their hearts were wrong. They received the kind of king they thought they wanted, yet Saul was ultimately a thorn in the nation's side. The nation needed a wise king whose heart and life were marked by devotion to true worship and the commands of Torah.

The Israelites would not drift into holiness, and neither would their king. They needed to love the Lord with their hearts, souls, and minds. They needed to fear Yahweh and trust what he had revealed. And they needed a better king than Saul. In the small town of Bethlehem, God was raising up such a young man.

Chapter Five

SINGING WITH A CHOIR OF WITNESSES

LYRICS GET INSIDE US. We know this is true because we have been in a car when someone puts on a song we have not heard in years, and suddenly the words come flowing back to our minds and out of our mouths. A melody has a penetrating power that must not be underestimated.

God has wired us in such a way that music speaks to us in the deep recesses of our being. How fitting, then, that an entire book of Scripture is a book of songs. The Psalms contain 150 chapters for our discipleship. Our souls will be stronger if we commit to learning and loving the Psalms.

In order to grow wise, we need to know what to sing.

A SINGING KING

Basically half of the Psalms were written by a man named David.[1] He became king over all Israel in approximately 1010 BC. The Lord had previously rejected Saul and sent Samuel to anoint Saul's successor. In 1 Samuel 16, Samuel sets

---

[1]This claim is based on a translation of the Hebrew as "of David," indicating authorship. For more on superscriptions in the Psalms, see Ian J. Vaillancourt, *Treasuring the Psalms: How to Read the Songs That Shape the Soul of the Church* (Downers Grove, IL: IVP Academic, 2023), 31-41.

apart young David to be Israel's future king. With David's indignation at Goliath's hubris and taunts (1 Sam 17:31-37), the reader can see that David is a man of conviction and courage.

In the years leading up to Saul's death, David is on the receiving end of Saul's jealousy and rage (1 Sam 18–26). He flees from Saul's snares and even spares Saul's life when the opportunity comes to take it. David's courage is coupled with wisdom. He is the kind of king that Israel needs.[2] In 2 Samuel 5, David becomes king over the whole land. Moreover, he is the first king from Judah's tribe (see Gen 49:10).

David knows how to fight, and he knows how to sing. These traits are important together because singing is warfare. Melodies are weapons of light against the darkness. In a world filled with deceit and false words, we need words to push back against the lies and to hold forth the truth like a lighthouse giving guidance to the ships at sea.

For forty years, David reigned as king. At the end of his life, 2 Samuel 23 reports these words as his last words:

> The oracle of David, the son of Jesse,
>   the oracle of the man who was raised on high,
> the anointed of the God of Jacob,
>   the sweet psalmist of Israel:
> "The Spirit of the LORD speaks by me;
>   his word is on my tongue.
> The God of Israel has spoken;
>   the Rock of Israel has said to me:
> When one rules justly over men,
>   ruling in the fear of God,
> he dawns on them like the morning light,
>   like the sun shining forth on a cloudless morning,
>   like rain that makes grass to sprout from the earth." (2 Sam 23:1-4)

The anointed king is a singing king. And through his words the Lord speaks. The words of the "sweet psalmist" are not just for himself; he is a psalmist of—and for—Israel. His words are for *their* lips, *their* hearts.

---

[2]By no means was David a flawless king. See 2 Sam 11–12 and Ps 51.

If David conducts himself as a faithful king and not just as a talented psalmist, the people will be abundantly blessed. Righteous rule leads to a flourishing people. The king, then, needs to rule "in the fear of God." Without the fear of the Lord, the king will not be wise. And without a king ruling wisely, the people will suffer. On the contrary, a God-fearing king will be a blessing to the people. God will shine on them like the dawning light and like refreshing rain (2 Sam 23:4). The right amounts of sun and rain will cause growth, such as grass sprouting from the earth (2 Sam 23:4). The people, too, need to grow. God is pleased to shine and rain his favor through a wise and righteous king.

David knew the connection between wisdom and blessing, and he knew that God's promise would outlast his own reign. In those last words found in 2 Samuel 23, David continues by saying:

> For does not my house stand so with God?
> For he has made with me an everlasting covenant,
>   ordered in all things and secure.
> For will he not cause to prosper
>   all my help and my desire?
> But worthless men are like thorns that are thrown away,
>   for they cannot be taken with the hand;
> but the man who touches them
>   arms himself with iron and the shaft of a spear,
>   and they are utterly consumed with fire. (2 Sam 23:5-7)

David's secure "house" refers to God's covenant in 2 Samuel 7. Nathan the prophet had conveyed divine words that the Lord was making a covenant with David, and this Davidic covenant was about a future offspring—or son—of David who would rule on the throne forever:

> When your days are fulfilled and you lie down with your fathers, I will raise up your offspring after you, who shall come from your body, and I will establish his kingdom. He shall build a house for my name, and I will establish the throne of his kingdom forever. . . . And your house and your kingdom shall be made sure forever before me. Your throne shall be established forever. (2 Sam 7:12-13, 16)

Near the end of David's life, his words confirm that he believed the promise of God. The Davidic house is ultimately secure, for God himself will establish a forever-king from David's line. Jesus is the Davidic king spoken about in 2 Samuel 7, and thus he is the one who fulfills and keeps this "everlasting covenant" that David spoke about in 2 Samuel 23. On the night Jesus is betrayed and arrested, he and his disciples sing a hymn before going to the Mount of Olives (Mt 26:30). Behold: a singing king who descended from a singing king.

THE GATEWAY INTO THE PSALTER

David's psalms are not organized in one spot. They are spread unevenly in the design of the Psalter. In total, seventy-three psalms have David's name in the superscription. But there are also anonymous psalms that are likely from David. We know, for instance, that Peter's comments in Acts 4 include a quote from Psalm 2, and Peter says the words are "through the mouth of our father David" (Acts 4:25). As another example, Psalm 9 and Psalm 10 are literarily and thematically connected, even though only Psalm 9 lists David's name in the superscription. If we should read Psalms 9 and Psalm 10 together, Psalm 10 is likely from David and lacks a superscription in order to reinforce the unity with the previous psalm.[3]

The opening of the Psalter consists not just of one psalm but of *two*. And like other psalms in the Psalter, Psalm 1 and Psalm 2 should be read together. They are thematically and linguistically connected.[4] Psalms 1–2 are two pillars forming the gateway into the Psalter, and through them we must travel if we are to read what the remainder of Books I through V have to offer.

Understanding these two foundational psalms will help us see the trajectory they set for the Psalter. The first word of Psalm 1 is a pronouncement of blessing, and the last line in Psalm 2 promises blessing for those who take refuge in the Anointed One. In Psalm 1 the focus is on "the man" whose ways

---

[3]Note that in the Septuagint, Ps 9 and Ps 10 comprise a single psalm. And if we look at the beginning of the lines of Ps 9 and Ps 10 in Hebrew, there is a general acrostic pattern that the psalms follow.
[4]See Robert L. Cole, *Psalm 1–2: Gateway to the Psalter*, Hebrew Bible Monographs (Sheffield, UK: Sheffield Phoenix Press, 2013); James M. Hamilton Jr. and Matthew Damico, *Reading the Psalms as Scripture* (Bellingham, WA: Lexham, 2024).

prosper, and in Psalm 2 the focus is on Israel's king who will rule the nations.[5] The wicked in Psalm 1 will perish like chaff, and the wicked in Psalm 2 will perish in their sinful way. These correspondences, among others, establish the unity of Psalms 1–2.

Psalm 1 teaches us about wisdom as it makes negative statements. The blessed person does not walk according to wicked counsel, does not stand in the path of rebellious sinners, and does not sit at the table of mockers. Positively, this person's delight is in God's law—the Torah. This person meditates on God's law day and night (Ps 1:2), a rhythm that signals devotion to the wisdom and commands in God's Word.

The result of a life immersed in truth is fruitfulness and vitality. This blessed figure "is like a tree planted by streams of water that yields its fruit in its season, and its leaf does not wither. In all that he does, he prospers" (Ps 1:3). This tree may recall Genesis 2, where the tree of life stood in the midst of the Garden of Eden. Though God barred his image bearers from Eden in Genesis 3, the imagery of Psalm 1 suggests that a kind of Edenic life is present in the heart of those who delight in the law of the Lord.

Blessedness is for the one who walks the path of life. But the wicked will not flourish under God's blessing; they will perish under God's wrath. In Psalm 1, the wicked and the sinners and the scoffers are groups who defy the Lord's wisdom. Their delight is not in what is good. Like the nations that rage in Psalm 2, the wicked oppose the Lord and reject his authority (Ps 2:1-3). In the minds of rebels, God's commands feel like unwanted constraints, bonds they want to burst apart (Ps 2:3).

Most seriously, the wicked are characterized by their opposition to the Lord's Anointed One—the Messiah (Ps 2:2). The psalmist says, "Now therefore, O kings, be wise; be warned, O rulers of the earth. Serve the LORD with fear, and rejoice with trembling. Kiss the Son, lest he be angry, and you perish in the way, for his wrath is quickly kindled. Blessed are all who take refuge in him" (Ps 2:10-12).

---

[5]Seen together, Ps 1–2 are ultimately about the Messiah, Israel's king. The promised Christ is the Blessed Man, the one whose ways prosper and whose heart delights in divine words. He will overcome his enemies and rule with righteousness. The enemies of Yahweh oppose the Christ in vain. They will perish in their folly.

The psalmist specifically invokes the language of wisdom ("be wise") and fear ("Serve the Lord with fear"). The wicked should abandon the path of the fool, and this repentance involves the embrace of the Messiah, "the Son" (Ps 2:12). To kiss the Son is a picture of allegiance and devotion. The problem with the wicked is that their hearts are not devoted to God. Their allegiance is elsewhere, to what is not God. For those who do kiss the Son, there is a promise: "Blessed are all who take refuge in him" (Ps 2:12). While conspiring against the Son will lead to experiencing God's wrath, finding refuge in the Son will lead to experiencing God's blessing.

The two gateway psalms should guide the reader's expectations of the whole Psalter. There is a path of life, and those on this path will flourish. The vitality of their lives is connected to where they have found refuge: they have fled to the Son. They reject the counsel of the wicked and the path of sinners. Their hope is in God's Messiah, the Davidic king. Their allegiance is to the one God will raise up on their behalf.

For the Psalms to make us wise, we need to be those who read with a view toward the blessed life and who understand that the blessed life is found in the Blessed Man. This Blessed Man is ultimately God's Son (Ps 1:1; 2:7). In the Blessed Man *we* are blessed. Our refuge in Christ means everlasting life. The Psalms invite us to thrive in the presence of God. They want us to expect the vindication of the righteous and the downfall of the wicked.

The psalmists are calling us to join the choir of witnesses who testify to God's covenant faithfulness and steadfast love. The wise walk the path of life with songs in their heart and on their lips.

THE HILL OF THE LORD

The goal of the path of life is communion with God, not just along the way but also as the destination itself. Because of God's greatness and holiness, think of approaching God as ascending into his presence. Since Jerusalem was a city on a hill, and since the temple was the place of divine worship for offerings and priestly mediation, the arrival of the worshiper was an ascent to the Lord.

The psalmist has this notion of ascending to God's presence in mind when he asks, "O Lord, who shall sojourn in your tent? Who shall dwell on your holy hill?" (Ps 15:1). The answer to the questions is about a person of blameless character: "He who walks blamelessly and does what is right and speaks truth in his heart; who does not slander with his tongue and does no evil to his neighbor, nor takes up a reproach against his friend" (Ps 15:2-3).

These moral descriptions are of a wise person. Fools do not love the truth, nor do they live according to it. The one who shall dwell on Yahweh's holy hill is someone "in whose eyes a vile person is despised, but who honors those who fear the LORD" (Ps 15:4). This worshiper loves what God loves and rejects what God rejects. This person does not delight in the wicked but delights in the objects of God's delight—those who fear the Lord.

In Psalm 15's opening verse, the writer asked, "Who shall dwell on your holy hill?" And we need to remember that the phrase "holy hill" appeared earlier in Book I of Psalms. According to Psalm 2, God has "set my King on Zion, my holy hill" (Ps 2:6). The expectation, then, is that God's Messiah is the holy one who shall dwell on the holy hill. The righteous redeemer can ascend the mountain of the Lord.

This same messianic answer fits with Psalm 24. There the psalmist asks, "Who shall ascend the hill of the LORD? And who shall stand in his holy place?" (Ps 24:3). The answer in the psalm is about a life above reproach: "He who has clean hands and a pure heart, who does not lift up his soul to what is false and does not swear deceitfully. He will receive blessing from the LORD and righteousness from the God of his salvation" (Ps 24:4-5).

The one who ascends the holy hill is identified near the end of Psalm 24: "Lift up your heads, O gates! And be lifted up, O ancient doors, that the King of glory may come in" (Ps 24:7). Here is the King whom God has set on his holy hill (Ps 2:6). This is the triumphant Messiah, the one who shall rule the nations, the one whose wise heart and blameless life ensure that he can dwell in the tent of the Lord.

In light of Psalm 2:12, what shall become of those who take refuge in the blessed Son of God? If the Son is the King who ascends the holy hill, then because of our union with the King, we too shall ascend. The hill of the Lord is the image of what we were made for: to commune with the true and living God. The reason wisdom leads to life is that this life is the life of God for his people.

THE SHADOW OF DEATH

As the wise learn to sing on their way to the new Jerusalem, they must learn to sing in the dark, in the valley.

Perhaps the most famous song in the Psalms begins like this: "The Lord is my shepherd; I shall not want. He makes me lie down in green pastures. He leads me beside still waters. He restores my soul. He leads me in paths of righteousness for his name's sake" (Ps 23:1-3). The Good Shepherd of our souls is faithful and trustworthy, caring for our souls and guiding us into blessing and nourishment.

But what happens when our eyes cannot see the hill of the Lord because we are in the valley of despair? The wise know they never walk alone. David says, "Even though I walk through the valley of the shadow of death, I will fear no evil, for you are with me; your rod and your staff, they comfort me. You prepare a table before me in the presence of my enemies; you anoint my head with oil; my cup overflows" (Ps 23:4-5).

Biblical wisdom involves recognizing the truth of God's abiding presence even when all signs in the shadows point to abandonment. We walk by faith and not by sight. This faith is why the psalmist ends Psalm 23 by saying, "Surely goodness and mercy shall follow me all the days of my life, and I shall dwell in the house of the Lord forever" (Ps 23:6).

The valley of the shadow of death is on the way to the hill of the Lord. The valley does not last forever; dwelling in the house of the Lord is what lasts forever. Because the psalmist is confident in God's ever-present help and the certain future of everlasting communion, he can persevere by faith and sing in the dark.

Sometimes the songs you hear do not come from your own lips. Have you ever heard someone call out in a deep valley? There is an echo because of the shape of the landscape. You could hear the echoes of someone's cry or someone's song—or both. When you find yourself unable to sing in the valley because your heart is bogged down in despair or bewilderment, listen to the echoes from those who have gone before you. The songs of the choir of witnesses can be heard echoing in the valley. The Psalms are their prayers and cries to God, echoing these many centuries later down to us.

The most common type of psalm is a lament. Given the frequency of this kind of psalm, we should expect that the path of wisdom will involve learning to endure the hardships of life in a fallen world. Part of Christian endurance will be trusting the Lord's providence and provision in our lives during such suffering. The lament psalms help disabuse us of the notion that there is no darkness along the path of the wise. The lament psalms confirm that God is light for us even when all else seems dark. He is with us and for us. He faithfully guides and delivers. He will bring us home to that shining city, and no shadowy valley will ever derail his sovereign purposes for us. The wise will learn that even in the valley, God is worthy of trust and worship.

LEARNING THE WAYS OF GOD

As God guides his people, he shepherds them by his word. In Psalms, the righteous care about God's words. They know the effect of his law on the heart when his law is internalized: "The law of the LORD is perfect, reviving the soul; the testimony of the LORD is sure, making wise the simple" (Ps 19:7).

The journey into wisdom is through divine instruction, and this instruction is present in the very words of Scripture. We are people who need divine instruction, so we are people who need Scripture. Ignoring Scripture is a surefire method for a life of folly. Wisdom is a life lived in conformity with the way God has made the world, and his Word speaks of these ways. If we are to learn the ways of God, then, we must meditate on Scripture.

Like the blessed person in Psalm 1, we need to meditate and reflect on it with delight (Ps 1:2). We need to believe the psalmist when he says that God's commands are more desirable than gold and sweeter than honey (Ps 19:10). In a cyclical way, the desirability of God's words will draw us to them, and being drawn to God's words will evermore reveal their desirability.

In Psalm 25, David prays what should be our prayer, for the sake of our growth in wisdom. He says, "Make me to know your ways, O LORD; teach me your paths. Lead me in your truth and teach me, for you are the God of my salvation; for you I wait all the day long" (Ps 25:4-5). The psalmist needed to be taught, as do we. The psalmist needed divine truth, as do we.

David says, "Good and upright is the LORD; therefore he instructs sinners in the way. He leads the humble in what is right, and teaches the humble his way. All the paths of the LORD are steadfast love and faithfulness, for those who keep his covenant and his testimonies" (Ps 25:8-10). Psalm 25:8 asserts that God instructs sinners because he himself is good. His bestowal of wisdom flows out of his character. And we know that this instruction will be upright because the Lord himself is good and upright.

What kind of people learn from God? David says that God "leads the humble in what is right, and teaches the humble his way" (Ps 25:9). The humble think much of God, not much of themselves. They extol God's righteousness and not their own. The humble trust God's promises and submit to his commands. They are not resistant to God's words. It is pride that resists the Lord. Our pride wants to be right and resists correction. Pride recoils against rebuke. It is humility that is willing to learn, to reevaluate the direction of one's feet on the path of life, and to repent of folly for the sake of life with God.

The psalmist asks, "Who is the man who fears the LORD? Him will he instruct in the way that he should choose" (Ps 25:12). Learners of God's ways are not only humble; they are those who fear the Lord. Reverence for God is not rooted in human pride. Pride obscures the eyes of our hearts that should behold God's greatness and worth. Humility enables spiritual sight that makes us wise because the humble are those who will fear the Lord and delight in his revelation.

According to the psalmist, those who fear the Lord are friends of the Lord: "The friendship of the LORD is for those who fear him, and he makes known to them his covenant" (Ps 25:14). God does not hold back the wise at arm's reach. He brings them close, to his very heart. He counsels them with his words and imparts wisdom to their minds. Covenant life with God means covenant friendship. And friendship with the Lord is not a passing thing. His friendship is forever.

God teaches us his ways because we are his friends. Do you not share things with your friends? Does communion between true friends not include disclosure and love and loyalty? If friendship with the Lord is good news in the old covenant, how much better is this news in the reality of the new covenant!

Jesus tells his disciples, "No longer do I call you servants, for the servant does not know what his master is doing; but I have called you friends, for all that I have heard from my Father I have made known to you" (Jn 15:15). The friends of Christ are those who trust him and follow him (Jn 15:14). He will demonstrate his love and faithfulness by laying down his own life, for there is no greater love than to lay down your life for your friends (Jn 15:13).

By learning the ways of Christ, the disciples have been learning the ways of God. The Lord Jesus has made known to them the kinds of things that will end up in the four Gospels. These disciples are his friends. And just as the psalmist teaches, the Lord makes known his covenant to those who fear him and follow him.

THE INTEGRITY OF THE WISE

God will vindicate his friends, and his friends believe this. The conviction about their vindication shows up in the words they speak during righteous suffering. These kind of psalms can sound bold because the psalmist asserts his integrity and innocence. But the idea is that the psalmist is innocent with regard to some accusation or assault that is underway.

Consider Psalm 26: "Vindicate me, O Lord, for I have walked in my integrity, and I have trusted in the Lord without wavering. Prove me, O Lord, and try me; test my heart and my mind. For your steadfast love is before my eyes, and I walk in your faithfulness" (Ps 26:1-3). Because the psalmist fears the Lord, he calls for the Lord to examine his heart. He knows that the Lord's examination will reveal the injustice of the accusations or assault.

Walking wisely produces a life of integrity. We know from several admissions that the speaker in Psalm 26 has been walking wisely: "I do not sit with men of falsehood, nor do I consort with hypocrites. I hate the assembly of evildoers, and I will not sit with the wicked" (Ps 26:4-5). David imitates the behavior of the Blessed Man in Psalm 1:1. David has avoided the ways and assembly of the wicked. He has said, "Teach me your way, O Lord, and lead me on a level path because of my enemies" (Ps 27:11).

David has experienced the provision and deliverance of the Lord in his life. He urges others to walk wisely that they may have these experiences as well: "Oh, taste and see that the Lord is good! Blessed is the man who takes refuge in him! Oh, fear the Lord, you his saints, for those who fear him have no lack!" (Ps 34:8-9).

According to David, fearing the Lord bears the fruit of obedience, and this fruit looks like turning from evil and pursuing what is good. The king says, "Come, O children, listen to me; I will teach you the fear of the LORD. What man is there who desires life and loves many days, that he may see good? Keep your tongue from evil and your lips from speaking deceit. Turn away from evil and do good; seek peace and pursue it" (Ps 34:11-14).

Walking wisely means pursuing what we know pleases the Lord and turning from what we know dishonors the Lord. This faithfulness is rooted in a heart that esteems and reveres the Lord. The heart of the wicked is not like this, but God's friends want to walk in integrity. They understand that false accusations or assaults may come, but they persevere in their integrity all the while knowing that God will vindicate his friends. David says, "By this I know that you delight in me: my enemy will not shout in triumph over me. But you have upheld me because of my integrity, and set me in your presence forever" (Ps 41:11-12).

A life of integrity is the opposite of hypocrisy. The hypocrite projects one thing outwardly even though a different state exists inwardly. Hypocrites, therefore, are not what they appear to be. But those who walk in integrity have lives that inwardly and outwardly match. Though not sinless, wise people truly trust God and want to live out a love for God in all of life.

CONCLUSION

The songs of Psalms matter for our growth in wisdom because these psalmists—and particularly David—turn to the Lord with their many prayers, and thus they show us how and why and when we should turn to the Lord. The psalmists tell of opponents who have risen against them, but they also lift up the rescuing power and grace of the Lord. They lament the sicknesses and sins that plague their bodies and hearts, but they also praise God's steadfast love and covenant friendship.

We need the Psalms because these writers do not turn from the Lord. They battle for hope, and they sing with faith. By joining the choir of psalmists, we add our voice to the chorus that shouts from mountaintops and echoes in deep valleys that God is worthy of praise and shepherds his people by his word and unto glory. Because the psalmists are wise, they know that the present distresses will not deny them their future in God's presence. God will dwell forever with his friends.

Whether expressing thanksgiving or bewilderment, pleas or praise, lament or remembrance, jubilation or confession, the psalmists teach us to keep turning to God. Since the promised King has ascended the hill of the Lord, we can rejoice that our path leads to the same place. This hill is our destination because this King is our savior. It is the kind of good news that makes you want to sing.

Chapter Six

WISDOM FOR ROYAL SONS AND DAUGHTERS

THINK OF THE THINGS YOU SEE little kids doing when they are playing together. You see things like blocks or kitchenware or plastic tools or crayons or dolls or board games or consoles or wrestling or racing or sports or some expression of make-believe. Creative and imaginative play is important for children if they are going to grow up to rule the world with wisdom. That kind of play is rehearsal for exercising dominion to the glory of God.

The Lord told his image bearers, "Be fruitful and multiply and fill the earth and subdue it, and have dominion over the fish of the sea and over the birds of the heavens and over every living thing that moves on the earth" (Gen 1:28). This commission to dominion is something fulfilled by those who rule over creation—ruling as kings and queens.

Wisdom is needed for God's royal sons and daughters to fulfill what he has made them for and called them to do. In order to reflect more on the art of living wisely in God's world, it is time to hear from Solomon.

SOLOMON'S PRAYER AND GOD'S ANSWER

David reigned as king over Israel for forty years, from approximately 1010 to 970 BC. His successor was his son Solomon, who reigned as king over Israel for forty years as well, from 970–930 BC. We read about Solomon's life in 1 Kings 1–11 and 2 Chronicles 1–9.

Before David's death, he tells his son, "I am about to go the way of all the earth. Be strong, and show yourself a man, and keep the charge of the LORD your God, walking in his ways and keeping his statutes, his commandments, his rules, and his testimonies, as it is written in the Law of Moses, that you may prosper in all that you do and wherever you turn" (1 Kings 2:2-3). David's last words to his son reflect the requirements for Israel's king laid out in Deuteronomy 17:14-20. Solomon needs to be a wise king, and wise kings love God's law. Wisdom is necessary not only for Solomon's well-being but also for the future of the nation.

The Lord says to Solomon in a dream, "Ask what I shall give you" (1 Kings 3:5). Solomon's request goes like this: "Give your servant therefore an understanding mind to govern your people, that I may discern between good and evil, for who is able to govern this your great people?" (1 Kings 3:9). Solomon's language evokes the notion of wisdom because discerning "between good and evil" is something the wise must be able to do. The Lord's response is to grant the request: "Behold, I give you a wise and discerning mind, so that none like you has been before you and none like you shall arise after you" (1 Kings 3:12).

The promise to Solomon is of supreme wisdom. None will be able to match his understanding (1 Kings 4:29-31). And his wisdom quickly becomes evident. When two women lay claimed to a child, Solomon discerns how to handle the situation (1 Kings 3:16-27). "And all Israel heard of the judgment that the king had rendered, and they stood in awe of the king, because they perceived that the wisdom of God was in him to do justice" (1 Kings 3:28).

Wisdom from God will show itself. Awareness about Solomon's wisdom increases, and the land lives under God's blessing. According to 1 Kings 4, the people "were as many as the sand by the sea. They ate and drank and were happy" (1 Kings 4:20). They "lived in safety, from Dan even to Beersheba, every man under his vine and under his fig tree, all the days of Solomon"

(1 Kings 4:25). These descriptions highlight a flourishing people under a wise king.

Part of Solomon's reign includes the creative output of proverbs and songs. The biblical author says, "He also spoke 3,000 proverbs, and his songs were 1,005" (1 Kings 4:32). Though we do not possess all of Solomon's proverbs and songs, we have the book of Proverbs and the Song of Songs, so we know some of his writings. His writings extol truth, goodness, and beauty in God's world. Through his words, he shepherds the people toward wisdom.

As a wise king, Solomon is like a new but better Adam. "He spoke of trees, from the cedar that is in Lebanon to the hyssop that grows out of the wall. He spoke also of beasts, and of birds, and of reptiles, and of fish" (1 Kings 4:33). The mention of trees and animals recalls Genesis 2, where God provided many trees and animals under Adam's dominion. The shadow of Adam, then, is evident in Solomon's reign. He displays his knowledge about plants and creatures, in addition to writing maxims and lyrics.

With such a wise king ruling over Israel, the people outside the land learn of him and want to hear him. "And the people of all nations came to hear the wisdom of Solomon, and from all the kings of the earth, who had heard of his wisdom" (1 Kings 4:34). The king of Tyre rejoices at Solomon's wisdom: "Blessed be the LORD this day, who has given to David a wise son to be over this great people" (1 Kings 5:7; see also 2 Chron 2:12). When the queen of Sheba travels to hear Solomon, "she came to test him with hard questions" (1 Kings 10:1), and "Solomon answered all her questions; there was nothing hidden from the king that he could not explain to her" (1 Kings 10:3). His wisdom is even greater than she imagined (1 Kings 10:6-7; see also 2 Chron 9:5-6).

As a new Adam and son of David, Solomon has wisdom that amazes and blesses all who stream to him. Never before has anyone heard a man with such understanding.

FATHER OF A CORPORATE SON

If we remember that Solomon "spoke 3,000 proverbs" during his reign (1 Kings 4:32), we should wonder what they are and for whom he spoke them. A proverb is a concise statement of wisdom, a pithy saying, a maxim. A proverb cannot say everything about a subject that can and should be said, but it certainly gets people thinking. A trustworthy proverb merits reflection and application.

Now, as far as Solomon's proverbs go, were they for him personally, like diary entries? Were they for the next-in-line descendant who needed to know how to rule wisely when the day of royal accession would come?

The existence of the book of Proverbs confirms an audience beyond the royal family. The nation of Israel was the corporate son of God (Ex 4:22), and therefore the king of Israel was the divine representative who would shepherd the people. Because Israel's shepherd-king needed to know and love the law of God (Deut 17:14-20), because the king needed to rule righteously and wisely, and because Solomon possessed wisdom surpassing that of anyone who had ever lived, the preservation of Solomon's proverbs was for the benefit of God's people.

Think of Solomon as a spiritual father for his corporate son, the Israelites. The content of Proverbs is the result of the greatest mind that had ever ruled, so the Israelites would benefit from knowing, preserving, studying, and applying Solomon's wisdom. Centuries after Solomon died, there were men of King Hezekiah who were copying Solomon's proverbs for preservation (Prov 25:1), and this action confirms the importance ascribed to what Solomon produced.[1]

The father-son dynamic is evident in the opening unit of the book, Proverbs 1–9, where there are a series of addresses from the father to his son—thus also from the king to his people. His plea is that his son will heed the voice of wisdom and turn from the voice of folly. Throughout this unit, the king highlights the benefits of wisdom and exposes the disastrous effects of folly. Honesty about these realities is vital for the young man's maturation, and it is evidence of the father's love for his son. Following the language and logic of the addresses in Proverbs 1–9, we can conclude that the primary audience of the book's wisdom is the young. Older believers can benefit from what Solomon teaches, but the author's hope is to reach the heart of the young with the book's beautiful truth.

---

[1] Prov 30–31 are not from Solomon.

When we point people to wisdom, we are loving them. When we warn people about the consequences of folly, we are loving them. When we explain to people what it looks like to walk in the fear of the Lord, we are loving them. The book of Proverbs exists because the father loves his son, the king loves his nation, and the Lord loves his people. The Lord is the greater father, and in Proverbs he addresses us—his children.

BEGINNING AND ENDING WITH FEAR

Before the king's first address to his son, the book has a prologue in Proverbs 1:1-7. The source of these proverbs is identified as Solomon (Prov 1:1), and then the benefits of wisdom (and the book of Proverbs) are laid out (Prov 1:2-6). The prologue ends with one of the most famous verses from the book: "The fear of the Lord is the beginning of knowledge; fools despise wisdom and instruction" (Prov 1:7). A similar statement appears in the final chapter of the big unit of Proverbs 1–9: "The fear of the Lord is the beginning of wisdom, and the knowledge of the Holy One is insight" (Prov 9:10).

A proper fear of Yahweh is foundational to a wise life. If someone lacks a proper heart posture toward the Lord, wise instruction will seem undesirable, unnecessary, even repulsive. Fools "*despise* wisdom and instruction" (Prov 1:7). In their arrogance, fools prefer their own way and sneer at the counsel of the wise. One of the goals for the father in the book is to expose the lies of sin and the consequences of folly. Without an attitude of reverence for God, the son will eventually leave the father's home and live out what is within his own heart. The father's speeches are an effort to faithfully steward conversations and seasons in the young man's life so that the voice of Wisdom prevails.

To live wisely, the son must "fear the Lord." This notion is an important theme in the book of Proverbs. Not only does it appear in the first and last chapters of Proverbs 1–9, but it appears in the first and last chapters of the book. In the penultimate verse of Proverbs, we read, "Charm is deceitful, and beauty is vain, but a woman who fears the Lord is to be praised" (Prov 31:30). Fearing Yahweh forms an *inclusio* (or frame) for the book. Furthermore, the notion of fearing the Lord appears throughout the book of Proverbs fourteen times.[2] Since fourteen is twice the number seven, and since seven symbolizes completeness or perfection, the fourteen occurrences of fearing the Lord suggest the organizer's forethought and deliberation with regard to that phrase. Everything in the book of Proverbs unfolds between the opening and ending emphases about fearing the Lord. This frame for the book establishes a worldview within which and through which all the intervening subjects are to be understood. The book of Proverbs is not merely a self-help manual, though we will help ourselves by heeding its wisdom. Proverbs is not simply a Christianized version of good insights for living well. Though there is wisdom in Proverbs that parallels what can be found in ancient non-Israelite texts, the theme of "fearing the Lord" insists that we take the message of this book in a deeply spiritual sense.[3]

We should not be surprised that non-Israelite texts contain helpful and true sayings. After all, we believe in God's common grace and in general revelation.[4] Sin has affected people's reasoning, but it has not prevented God's image bearers from seeing anything true or good. For instance, non-believers have been able to discern the importance of financial stewardship and hard work. Watching the ant's ways can be a lesson to the sluggard (Prov 6:6), and an ant is not special revelation. However, all wisdom is ultimately from the Lord, because common grace and general revelation have their source in him.

The wisdom for Israel is framed by the fear of the Lord. A person who can discern truth in creation is limited when that person rejects the Creator. As James Hamilton puts it, "Proverbs has affinities with other ancient Near Eastern wisdom literature, but the theological content of the book is

---

[2]For those fourteen occurrences, see Prov 1:7, 29; 2:5; 8:13; 9:10; 10:27; 14:27; 15:16, 33; 16:6; 19:23; 22:4; 23:17; 31:30.
[3]In Egyptian and Mesopotamian literature, there are subjects and proverbial statements similar to what we read in Proverbs. According to Longman, "In terms of form, the proverb, which is the staple particularly of the second part of the book of Proverbs (Prov 10–31), is common in early Sumerian, Akkadian, Aramaic, and especially Egyptian literature. On the level of the whole book, probably the closest parallel is with the instructional literature of Egypt." Tremper Longman III, *The Fear of the Lord Is Wisdom: A Theological Introduction to Wisdom in Israel* (Grand Rapids, MI: Baker Academic, 2017), 156.
[4]By "general revelation," I am referring to how God's design and order in creation can establish insights about what helps or harms human flourishing.

synonymous with the theological content of the Pentateuch, and especially Deuteronomy."[5]

A truly wise life—the kind of wisdom the biblical authors are concerned about—is the overflow of a heart that seeks to know and walk with God.

In fact, let's think about the way we walk.

THE WAY WE WALK

When the biblical authors address the way we walk, they do not have in mind a swagger or a pace. They have in mind a *path*. The way we walk is the path we are on, and not all paths lead to the same place.

In the father's first address to his son, he envisions wicked people who may want the son to join their wicked deeds. So he says, "My son, do not walk in the way with them; hold back your foot from their paths, for their feet run to evil, and they make haste to shed blood" (Prov 1:15-16). In keeping with a purpose for the book to instill "prudence to the simple" and "knowledge and discretion to the youth" (Prov 1:4), the young man's growth in discernment will mean the ability to identify temptations and expose the evil path associated with them.

If the son makes his way the way of the wicked, he will share the destiny at the end of their path. The father knows this, which is why he says, "These men lie in wait for their own blood; they set an ambush for their own lives" (Prov 1:18). Young people are notoriously known for not thinking through the consequences of their decisions, so the father loves his son by helping him do that very thing. He imagines with his son a scenario and dialogue and a temptation. Then he helps his son think about where the path leads— and it leads to destruction. Since temptation never presents sin honestly, the father declares the disastrous end for those who walk the path of folly.

The father's hope is that after having greater clarity about wickedness and where it leads, the son will desire the path of life and blessing. He tells his

---

[5]James M. Hamilton Jr., *God's Glory in Salvation Through Judgment: A Biblical Theology* (Wheaton, IL: Crossway, 2010), 291. Longman concurs: "There is, accordingly, no way that the Israelite sages who produced Proverbs, Job, and Ecclesiastes would think that ancient Near Eastern wisdom teachers were wise in the most important sense of the word. After all, the latter are ignorant of the most important and basic truth of the cosmos" (Longman, *Fear of the Lord*, 161).

son that God "is a shield to those who walk in integrity" (Prov 2:7). While God opposes the wicked, he is a defender of his people. He is "watching over the way of his saints" (Prov 2:8). On the path of wisdom, the son will enjoy the shepherding care of God, who shall bestow understanding and deliver him from evil.

Walking the way of wisdom will mean more than following the father's instruction. It will involve trusting the heavenly Father's will and revelation. The father says, "Trust in the LORD with all your heart, and do not lean on your own understanding. In all your ways acknowledge him, and he will make straight your paths" (Prov 3:5-6). This is the equivalent in Proverbs to what Moses told the Israelites in Deuteronomy 6, to love the Lord with all their heart, soul, and might (Deut 6:5). The son must not seek to live on bread alone but on every word that comes from the mouth of God. And his father's mouth aims to faithfully communicate those words.

Since the son will live out what he trusts, he needs to trust the Lord to walk wisely. If he will live with inner regard and esteem for Yahweh, he will live out a love for God in all of life.

LIGHT FROM DEUTERONOMY

The father tells his son to trust God with his whole heart (Prov 3:5). That instruction, and other places in Proverbs as well, has the book of Deuteronomy looming in the background. In fact, if we are to properly understand the role that Proverbs is to play in the life of the king's son and the king's people, we need the illuminating light of Deuteronomy.

From Deuteronomy 1 and onward, clusters of terms—such as *commands, instruction, teaching, counsel, precepts, words*—appear throughout Deuteronomy as Moses seeks to lay out instruction for the new generation of Israelites who are preparing to inherit the land. Moses is concerned that they do not forget the Lord. In Proverbs, the father says, "My son, do not forget my teaching, but let your heart keep my commandments" (Prov 3:1). If the son forgets his father's teaching, he will forget the Lord, because his father's instruction is from and based on the Word of God.

In Deuteronomy 6:6-7, Moses told the Israelites, "And these words that I command you today shall be on your heart. You shall teach them diligently to your children, and shall talk of them when you sit in your house, and when you walk by the way, and when you lie down, and when you rise." One way to describe the father in Proverbs is as someone fulfilling the injunctions of Moses. The father is diligently teaching his son, talking about and applying God's commands to his son's life. The father—simultaneously a king—is instructing his son in the home, and, more broadly, the king is instructing the household of the nation.

The father's instruction references the Promised Land in ways that evoke Deuteronomy. He says, "For the upright will inhabit the land, and those with integrity will remain in it, but the wicked will be cut off from the land, and the treacherous will be rooted out of it" (Prov 2:21-22). Moses told the Israelites these very truths. The Israelites were to keep God's commands so that they "may live long in the land that the LORD swore to your fathers to give to them and to their offspring, a land flowing with milk and honey" (Deut 11:9). But if the Israelites rejected God's covenant stipulations, "then the anger of the LORD will be kindled against you, and he will shut up the heavens, so that there will be no rain, and the land will yield no fruit, and you will perish quickly off the good land that the LORD is giving you" (Deut 11:17).

The biblical authors tell of the Lord's corrective discipline in the lives of the Israelites. The Israelites experienced his chastisement as a result of their rebellion. Yet the Lord's discipline was rooted in his steadfast covenant love. Solomon says, "My son, do not despise the LORD's discipline or be weary of his reproof, for the LORD reproves him whom he loves, as a father the son in whom he delights" (Prov 3:11-12). The son should heed the Lord's corrective discipline, a posture that the nation itself was to adopt in the Old Testament. Moses told them, "Know then in your heart that, as a man disciplines his son, the LORD your God disciplines you. So you shall keep the commandments of the LORD your God by walking in his ways and by fearing him" (Deut 8:5-6).

The reason we have the book of Proverbs is the king's application of the book of Deuteronomy for the life of his son and his nation.

WISDOM AND THE TREE OF LIFE

Deuteronomy is not the only book from the Pentateuch that is in the background of Proverbs. Genesis is a source for the phrase "tree of life" that appears four times in Proverbs (Prov 3:18; 11:30; 13:12; 15:4). The only two books in the Old Testament with the phrase "tree of life" are Genesis and Proverbs, so the occurrences of the phrase in Proverbs are a deliberate callback to Genesis. The "tree of life" is first mentioned in Genesis 2:9, where God planted a garden in Eden and put the tree of life in the midst of it. In Genesis 3, Adam and Eve were exiled and then barred from reentering Eden so that Adam could not "reach out his hand and take also of the tree of life and eat, and live forever" (Gen 3:22). After Genesis 3:22, the tree of life is not mentioned again until the book of Proverbs. So why does Solomon bring it up? Because wisdom is related to life with God, and life with God is what we were made for. In fact, the path of wisdom is called a path "of life" and "peace" (Prov 2:19; 3:17; 5:6).

Let's consider the four occurrences of the "tree of life" in Proverbs.

The first occurrence is in Proverbs 3:18. There Solomon is talking about wisdom when he says, "She is a tree of life to those who lay hold of her; those who hold her fast are called blessed." He uses "tree of life" to mean the life-giving effects of wisdom. Those who find wisdom are blessed; they are spiritually enlivened, as if they were eating from the tree of life.

The second occurrence is in Proverbs 11:30. Solomon says, "The fruit of the righteous is a tree of life, and whoever captures souls is wise." The word *fruit* has in view the actions the righteous perform and the resulting impact. The decisions of the righteous have consequences, and these consequences are good. Because the righteous pursue what is good, the fruit of their actions is life giving to others—like "a tree of life."

The third occurrence is in Proverbs 13:12. Solomon teaches, "Hope deferred makes the heart sick, but a desire fulfilled is a tree of life." This verse is about what happens to the heart when the fulfillment of hope is prolonged or when a desire is fulfilled. When hope is deferred, the heart is saddened. But the heart is thrilled, full of life, when a desire is met. The phrase "tree of life" denotes a rejuvenated state of the heart.

The fourth occurrence is in Proverbs 15:4. Solomon says, "A gentle tongue is a tree of life, but perverseness in it breaks the spirit." This proverb is about how our words can affect others. We can build up or destroy, edify or tear down. A twisted (or perverse) tongue breaks the spirit of another person, but a gentle tongue is "a tree of life" to another person. Our wise words bear good fruit that others taste and are thereby nourished.

In Genesis, the "tree of life" is the tree with fruit that gives life, that spiritually nourishes. Because wisdom is life giving for the one who has wisdom, and because the acts of the righteous are life giving to those around them, and because the fulfillment of godly desires are life giving to the one with those desires, and because wise words are life giving to those who hear them, Solomon employs the Edenic "tree of life" image to make his lifegiving point.

Though we are not in Eden and have no access to the actual tree of life that was in the midst of the garden, we can pursue wisdom and live wisely before the Lord. The echoes of Eden are experienced as we grow in the fear of the Lord and walk uprightly on the path of life that is truly life. Matthew Henry connects the lives of the saints with the tree of life. He says,

> The righteous are as *trees of life*; fruits of their piety and charity, their instructions, reproofs, examples, and prayers, their interest in heaven, and their influence upon earth, are like the fruits of that tree, precious and useful, contributing to the support and nourishment of the spiritual life in many; they are the ornaments of paradise, God's church on earth, for whose sake it stands.[6]

THE VOICES OF WISDOM AND FOLLY

When the phrase "tree of life" appears for the first time in Proverbs, it is equated with wisdom. But more is going on than just an equative statement. Wisdom is called "she" and "her." Solomon says, "She is a tree of life to those who lay hold of her; those who hold her fast are called blessed" (Prov 3:18). He ascribes personal qualities to wisdom, using the literary device of personification.

Personified wisdom in Proverbs is a woman to cling to (Prov 3:18). She is also a voice to heed, but hers is not the only voice calling for a hearing. Proverbs presents the contrasting voices of Lady Wisdom and Lady Folly.

In Proverbs 1, Lady Wisdom calls to the people in the street and in the market (Prov 1:20-21). She wants people to turn at her reproof and receive

---

[6]Matthew Henry, *Matthew Henry's Commentary on the Whole Bible*, vol. 3, *Job to Song of Solomon* (Old Tappan, NJ: Revell), 855.

her spirit and words (Prov 1:23). But she has stretched out her hands to people who refused to listen (Prov 1:24). When disaster comes on fools, Lady Wisdom will not answer their cry because she will not be found (Prov 1:26-28). But whoever heeds her words will dwell secure, and disaster will not overtake them (Prov 1:33).

The son in the book needs to understand that his father's instructions are really the greater voice of Lady Wisdom, who will give life and blessing to all who seek her. Her gain is better than any worldly riches (Prov 3:14-15). She has pleasant ways and peaceful paths for those who come to her (Prov 3:17). The son should value and esteem wisdom, embracing her with devotion (Prov 4:6-8). Nothing can compare with her (Prov 3:15; 8:11), especially since she offers long life to those who fear the Lord (Prov 3:16).

The voice of Lady Folly is not what it appears to be. Her words are smooth but deadly (Prov 2:16). Her promises are false and take the listener down the road to death (Prov 2:18-19). While Lady Folly presents sin as desirable, she does not tell the truth. She diminishes the possibility of consequences and exaggerates the pleasure of rebellion. She does not care what happens to those who listen to her lies. "Her feet go down to death; her steps follow the path to Sheol; she does not ponder the path of life; her ways wander, and she does not know it" (Prov 5:5-6).

Because Lady Folly does not advertise that her ways lead to death, she is deceptive. So the father tells his son, "Keep your way far from her, and do not go near the door of her house" (Prov 5:8). The deceptive words of Lady Folly are especially evident in sexual temptation. The father wants his son to know ahead of time about her wily ways: "Say to wisdom, 'You are my sister,' and call insight your intimate friend, to keep you from the forbidden woman, from the adulteress with her smooth words" (Prov 7:4-5). He wants his son to know what she has done to others: "Let not your heart turn aside to her ways; do not stray into her paths, for many a victim has she laid low, and all her slain are a mighty throng. Her house is the way to Sheol, going down to the chambers of death" (Prov 7:25-27).

As Proverbs presents the contrasting voices of Lady Wisdom and Lady Folly, we not only hear about their respective invitations, but we also glimpse the end of their respective paths. And glimpsing the end should help the son—and us—consider whether the path we are on is leading to a place we desire. Lady Folly's words lead to the chambers of death. Lady Wisdom, however, will lead her adherents to life everlasting.

The personification of Lady Wisdom is particularly strong in Proverbs 8. The Lord has had wisdom from the very beginning (Prov 8:22-23). His creative works were done by wisdom, and nothing he made was made without wisdom (Prov 8:24-31). Genesis 1 is a report of God's orderly work in the world he created, and Proverbs 8:22-31 confirms this truth through poetic language.

At the end of Proverbs 8, the dichotomy of the two paths is clear in Lady Wisdom's words: "For whoever finds me finds life and obtains favor from the Lord, but he who fails to find me injures himself; all who hate me love death" (Prov 8:35-36).

THE WAY LIFE TYPICALLY WORKS

When the biblical author promises life and blessing for the wise, and when he threatens distress and death for the fool, readers might conclude that the wise will walk an easier and more fruitful *earthly* path. For example, Solomon says, "Whoever walks in integrity walks securely, but he who makes his ways crooked will be found out" (Prov 10:9).

An interpretive danger to avoid when reading through Proverbs is expecting earthly fulfillment of these promises in an absolutizing sense, as if life were not complicated and inexplicable things did not happen. Do the righteous not suffer? Do the wicked not sometimes prosper? Do people who walk with integrity not still face obstacles? Do the wise not sometimes die young? Do the wicked sometimes not seem to get away with their schemes and escape consequences? Consider the earthly ministry of Jesus. The wicked came against him with conspiracy and intrigue. He, the holy and righteous one, was killed. His vindication occurred through his bodily resurrection—a kind of resurrection that comprises our hope when Jesus returns.

We can affirm two things: the book of Proverbs is true, and life is complicated. The proverbs are statements about how life typically works. There is order in God's world, so we would expect that those who work hard and with integrity will provide for themselves and those in their household. We would expect sluggardly people to struggle consistently. We would expect those who cut corners in order to acquire unjust gain will be exposed or, at the very least, experience the emptiness of the wealth they thought would satisfy them.

Proverbs is an exploration of what an ordered life in God's world should look like. Because facing temptations and evil is part of this earthly life, there are times when life seems to be the exception to what certain proverbs state. We must keep in mind, then, that the proverbs are general sayings.

Given the principial nature of Proverbs, we should make our decisions based on what would be in keeping with order in God's world. Since Proverbs 10:2 says, "Treasures gained by wickedness do not profit," we should take that truth as an exhortation toward faithful and disciplined work that avoids unrighteous shortcuts. Gain wealth in a manner that honors the Lord and does not sin against your neighbor. Since Proverbs 6:10-11 says, "A little sleep, a little slumber, a little folding of the hands to rest, and poverty will come upon you like a robber, and want like an armed man," we should assume that rejecting the responsibility to work will have negative financial consequences. Do not be lazy, because sluggardliness is self-destructive. Since Proverbs 13:21 says, "Disaster pursues sinners, but the righteous are rewarded with good," we should trust that wise decisions will lead to blessing, while foolish decisions will reap hardship.

We do not know what the future holds, so we should do what honors the Lord and demonstrates love toward our neighbor. Avoid unrighteous anger and rash behavior. Do not believe the lies of a seductress or the lusts in your heart. Work hard and with integrity, refusing to compromise your character with unethical shortcuts that hold the prospect for greater and quicker wealth. Believe that living foolishly will not improve your life in any way; rather, folly compounds the challenges for your life and in your relationships with others.

Though the proverbs should not be understood as absolute promises, the proverbs are still trustworthy guidance for the decisions and plans that God's people make in God's world.

CONCLUSION

When people think about where wisdom passages occur in Scripture, perhaps no book comes to mind more than Proverbs. Proverbs is a quintessential wisdom text because it contains thirty-one chapters of maxims for living in the fear of the Lord.

The proverbs should not be reduced to self-help material. Framed by the theme of fearing the Lord, Proverbs is a guide for faithful living in God's world. It aims our words and actions toward what would honor God and bless our neighbor. Solomon's words were for his son and for his nation. Through Solomon's words, the Lord is still shepherding the people of God on the path of life. God's people are a corporate son who is being trained to rule and exercise dominion.

In this world there are deceptive words to reject, lies to expose, sins to mortify, and temptations to overcome. To properly rule over our own hearts, we need wisdom. And to have wisdom, we need the fear of the Lord. Reverence for God is vital for living as faithful image bearers whose destiny is everlasting life. The voice of Lady Folly will not lead you there. She lures her listeners into the chambers of death. But the voice of Lady Wisdom calls to us even now. She loves the truth and speaks the truth. In her hand is life, and in her home is peace.

Chapter Seven

COVENANT LOVE FOR COVENANT PEOPLE

OF ALL THE OLD TESTAMENT BOOKS where wisdom is found, Proverbs may be the most popular, but the Song of Songs is the most difficult and disputed. When people read Solomon's famous song, they might see it as nothing more than poetic reflections of a couple's mutual desire and sexual intimacy. That kind of content is certainly present in the book, for chapter after chapter extols the sexual love between the man and the woman.

But as a book in the biblical canon, the Song of Songs should be read with the same assumptions that we bring to other canonical texts. We should assume that the Song of Songs is in touch with the biblical story line, that it instructs the people of Israel in their true worship of—and hope in—the living God, and that the ultimate meaning of what is going on in the song becomes clear in the canonical light of Christ and his church.

As we walk wisely in God's world, we will find that we are in a covenant relationship of life and love, and that this divine communion overcomes and surpasses even the greatest and deepest of earthly relationships and pleasures.

COVENANT LIFE

The living God made living creatures, so their life derives from him. This life is more than physical. In covenant with Yahweh, not only are we image bearers with the breath of life from God, but we also depend on God for our spiritual state and well-being.

In Genesis 2, God gave his creatures the "breath of life" (Gen 2:7) and then gave them the "tree of life" (Gen 2:9). As the representative of humanity, Adam was in covenant with God. Adam received the command of God and the warning if it was rejected (Gen 2:16-17). When he sinned against the Lord, his disobedience affected those he represented—*everyone* (Rom 5:12-21). God exiled Adam from Eden, effectively barring him from the tree of life (Gen 3:22-24).

We learn from Genesis 2 that life with God is a life in covenant with God. If the covenant members rejected God's commands, they would face death: "In the day that you eat of it you shall surely die" (Gen 2:17). After reading about the exile in Genesis 3, we might wonder whether hope remains for God's image bearers to return to their first home, to the Garden of Eden.

Though Eden was mentioned in the opening chapters of the Bible and then left behind, the reader of Solomon's song is transported there through the poetic scenes and dialogue of a woman and her beloved. This song extols love, and that is one of the reasons this song has captured the imaginations of readers throughout the centuries. The context for this love is paradise, a garden atmosphere, blossoming vines and fruitful land.

The Song of Songs does not use the word *Eden*, but the concepts and descriptions in the song are a literary portal to an ancient sanctuary where a man and a woman dwelled together naked and unashamed.

In eight chapters, readers can see the power and beauty of covenant life. The language in the song feels idyllic, transcendent, something that not even the historical Solomon's life could live up to. We know Solomon wrote songs because of what 1 Kings tells us: "He also spoke 3,000 proverbs, and his songs were 1,005" (1 Kings 4:32). But the biblical Song of Songs is not just any of his compositions, randomly chosen for a canonical collection. The opening verse calls the work "The Song of Songs, which is Solomon's" (Song 1:1). The superlative "Song of Songs" elevates this work above his other compositions.

The phrase does not diminish his other writings, but it does lift up the Song of Songs to a level of unparalleled importance.

Behold, then, the greatest song Solomon composed. What kinds of themes run throughout these chapters? Covenant life and love. God has made his people to dwell in his presence, and this hope is stirred by the Edenic context of a man and woman as they speak with figurative, provocative, and beautiful words.

THE GOODNESS OF MARRIAGE

At the center of the song is a wedding and the wedding night (Song 3:6–5:1).[1] In Song of Songs 3:6-11, we read of the king's arrival for the ceremony. He goes through the wilderness and arrives to make a covenant (Song 3:6, 11).

The marriage covenant is the context for the sexual intimacy and provocative language of the couple. The center of the song is not the only unit in the book with a marital covenant context, but it is the only unit that explicitly refers to "the day of his wedding" (Song 3:11).

A marriage context is evident at the opening of the song, when the woman declares her desire to kiss the man and to follow him into the bedchambers (Song 1:2-4). There are sections that recall life before marriage, such as his pronouncement that the season for marital love had arrived and that the time for separation had drawn to a close (Song 2:8-13). But there are multiple scenes in the book that are best interpreted as covenantal scenes of mutual desire and love. For example, she calls for raisins and apples (Song 2:5), which in the ancient world were thought to be aphrodisiacs. And she describes his position as having his left hand under her head and his right hand embracing her (Song 2:6). These scenes occur in the song before the central unit (Song 3:6–5:1), but they are still covenant contexts for the couple's words and love.

The Song of Songs does not celebrate lust and immorality. It celebrates the goodness of the marriage covenant. Marriage was God's idea in Genesis 1–2, where he commanded his image bearers to be fruitful and multiply and

---

[1] The wedding and wedding night are part of a unit at the center of the song's chiastic arrangement. The outer frame is Song 1:1–2:7 and Song 8:5-14, the penultimate units are Song 2:8–3:5 and Song 5:2–8:4, and the middle of the song is Song 3:6–5:1.

exercise dominion. The garden life of the first couple is echoed in Solomon's song, where we read of a married couple enjoying the delightful union of their covenant life.

The author of Hebrews says, "Let marriage be held in honor among all, and let the marriage bed be undefiled, for God will judge the sexually immoral and adulterous" (Heb 13:4). Though Solomon himself did not avoid all sexual immorality, his song lifts high the covenant of marriage and holds it in honor.

Even the speech of the couple has observable transitions when the marriage covenant is the context for the words. When the woman or the man uses metaphors to speak provocatively of the other's body, these words do not occur in a premarriage setting. We learn from their example that the words from the man to the woman, or vice versa, must be appropriate. Before marriage, he speaks of her lovely cheeks and neck (Song 1:10). Before marriage, he speaks of her sweet voice and lovely face (Song 2:14). Within their marriage, he and she speak to one another with language that would awaken desire and intimacy, language appropriate within a covenant between a husband and a wife.

The Song of Songs portrays an undefiled marriage bed. This couple is devoted to each other. The man declares that the woman is a lily among brambles (other women), and she pronounces him an apple tree among the trees (other men) of the forest (Song 2:2-3). The depictions of the setting for love mention things such as anointing oils (Song 1:3), myrrh (Song 1:13), henna blossoms (Song 1:14), cedar beams (Song 1:17), and beds of spices (Song 6:2). These terms cluster together to evoke a sense of allurement and delight. The images support the larger notion of the goodness of marriage.

There are scenes of separation and renewal in the Song (see Song 3:1-5; 5:2–8:4), so the portrayal of the goodness of marriage does not deny inevitable difficulties. The couple must address "the little foxes that spoil the vineyards" (Song 2:15). But the couple's devotion to each other gives them endurance for the difficulties. The book ends on the note of anticipation and desire (Song 8:13-14).

We need to believe the Bible's portrayal of marriage. We live among cultural forces that contort and undermine the biblical truth and beauty of marriage.

God created marriage to be between one man and one woman, and any other alleged marriage arrangement is dishonorable before God. Deviating from God's design will not be good for your neighbor or your society. When sexual pursuits and activity are disconnected from the covenant of marriage, sinful pursuits and rebellion are underway. And rebelling against the Lord and his design will not help you or your neighbor.

Wisdom involves agreeing with what the Bible teaches about things. And the biblical authors teach God's design and blessings for marriage.[2]

THE PROPER TIME TO AWAKEN LOVE

What about those who are not married? How should they live with regard to sexual desire and intimacy? The answers to these questions are clear when the Song of Songs incorporates a group known as "the daughters of Jerusalem."

The first time "the daughters of Jerusalem" are mentioned is in Song of Songs 1:5, where the woman (in a premarriage context) speaks to them about her own appearance. She addresses them again in Song of Songs 2:7 (this time in the context of her marriage) with an exhortation: "I adjure you, O daughters of Jerusalem, by the gazelles or the does of the field, that you not stir up or awaken love until it pleases," an exhortation she repeats in Song of Songs 3:5; 8:4.[3]

These daughters are unmarried, and the woman warns them against awakening love before the proper time ("until it pleases"). The pleasing or proper time for love is the covenant of marriage, and this truth is confirmed by the couple's activity in the song. The words and scenes of intimacy are in covenant contexts. Learning to think wisely about sexuality, the daughters of Jerusalem must exercise self-control and not awaken sexual love outside the covenant of marriage.

Self-control is no easy exhortation in a world rife with sexual temptation. But because of how God designed marriage and human flourishing, sexual

---

[2] See Ray Ortlund, *Marriage and the Mystery of the Gospel*, Short Studies in Biblical Theology (Wheaton, IL: Crossway, 2016); Brad Wilcox, *Get Married: Why Americans Must Defy the Elites, Forge Strong Families, and Save Civilization* (New York: Broadside Books, 2024).
[3] In the literary structure of the book, the woman's exhortation to the "daughters of Jerusalem" is something that draws units to a close in Song 2:7; 3:5; 8:4.

self-control outside the marriage covenant is vital. Embracing God's design for marriage is an act of trust and submission to God's wisdom, sovereignty, and goodness. This embrace will mean a countercultural life because the instincts of sinners are to seek quick fulfillment of their desires. Yet in a fallen world, sin has affected our hearts and minds. A desire *for* something does not mean that thing is good or beneficial. Temptation offers us lies to believe, such as the lie that nothing should get in the way of what we want, or that something is not be bad if we have the desire for it, or that what we pursue should just be our business and nobody else's, or that others should affirm how we want to live if they really love us, or that getting what we desire will be best for us.

The biblical authors prioritize self-control over self-expression. They want God's image bearers to consider objective realities of right and wrong, good and evil, wisdom and folly. A major reason that the unmarried daughters of Jerusalem should conduct themselves with self-control is the objective goodness of God's design for men and women and for marriage itself.

In addition to the temptation of sexual immorality with others outside the covenant of marriage, consider the rampant use of pornography. Indulgence in pornography leads to the erosion of virtue and the cultivation of vice. If the woman in Solomon's song warns against awakening love until the proper time, then we can conclude that pornography would be an example of sexual immorality and thus forbidden under her warning.[4] Her words are like Lady Wisdom's voice, leading listeners toward blessing and away from destruction.

Young men need to model self-control. Paul tells Timothy, "Let no one despise you for your youth, but set the believers an example in speech, in conduct, in love, in faith, in purity" (1 Tim 4:12). And he tells Titus, "Urge the younger men to be self-controlled" (Titus 2:6). The cultivation of sexual self-control will be crucial for their holiness and for the responsibilities and relationships in their lives.

Paul tells Timothy to treat "younger women as sisters, in all purity" (1 Tim 5:2). Men should treat women with respect and dignity, with pure words and unreproachable behavior. Near the end of Solomon's song, there

---

[4] See Ray Ortlund, *The Death of Porn: Men of Integrity Building a World of Nobility* (Wheaton, IL: Crossway, 2021).

are voices that say, "We have a little sister, and she has no breasts. What shall we do for our sister on the day when she is spoken for? If she is a wall, we will build on her a battlement of silver, but if she is a door, we will enclose her with boards of cedar" (Song 8:8-9). These voices are protective.

Since men are to treat other women as sisters, a natural application would be the intent to protect and preserve their dignity and honor. The words and actions of those in the Song are edifying and not demeaning, dignifying and not harmful. The characters in the lyrics are showing us how things ought to be. Solomon wrote the song for readers outside Eden, yet the content of the song fills our imaginations with Edenic senses and hopes. Folly corrupts lovely things. We need wisdom to call "good" what God has made good and to expose the lies that would undermine it.

THE PARABLE OF MARRIAGE

The reason that Edenic senses reverberate through Solomon's song is that the covenant love of the couple points beyond a human marriage. This truth is one of the most important to notice in the song, yet it is also among the most controversial. The long-standing interpretation in Jewish tradition and in the history of Christian interpretation is that the husband-wife union points to the relationship between God and his people. From a new covenant standpoint, we would say that the husband and wife point to the joyful union between Christ and his bride—the church.

Marriage is a parable, and God designed it that way. When Paul writes about marriage in Ephesians 5, he says, "This mystery is profound, and I am saying that it refers to Christ and the church" (Eph 5:32). But this is not just Paul's idea. During the days of Jesus' ministry, John the Baptist said, "You yourselves bear me witness, that I said, 'I am not the Christ, but I have been sent before him.' The one who has the bride is the bridegroom. The friend of the bridegroom, who stands and hears him, rejoices greatly at the bridegroom's voice. Therefore this joy of mine is now complete" (Jn 3:28-29). John is the friend of the bridegroom, and he has heard the bridegroom's voice. The Lord Jesus has come for his bride.

The parabolic purpose of marriage is rooted in the Old Testament. The Israelites entered a covenant with Yahweh at Mount Sinai, and later biblical authors refer to Yahweh as the husband and the nation as the covenant wife (Ex 24:8; Is 54:5; Jer 2:2; Ezek 16:8). The existence of this covenant is confirmed when the prophets charge the Israelites with committing spiritual adultery as they abandoned Yahweh and pursued idols (Jer 3:8; 31:32; Hos 1:2). The prophet Hosea was to marry a woman of unfaithfulness in order to display, through his marriage, the theological truth about Yahweh's relationship with Israel: Yahweh was in covenant with an unfaithful people (Hos 1:2–2:3).

Coming to the Song of Songs, we read of a man and woman in the covenant of marriage. Are there clues in the song that connect the content to the people of Israel and even to what precedes the Israelites?

First, consider that the song was written by the son of David and is preserved for God's people. The author is not anonymous, and the audience is not ambiguous. References to the king (Song 1:4) and Jerusalem (Song 1:5) and Solomon (Song 1:5) are examples early in the book of connections to the Israelites.

Second, there are allusions to the Promised Land. Fig trees and vines are fruitful (Song 2:13). Livestock are thriving (Song 4:1-2). The Hebrew words for the phrase "scarlet thread" (Song 4:3) appear in one other place in the Old Testament—Joshua 2:18, where Rahab hangs a "scarlet cord" in her window in Jericho, which is the first place the Israelites conquered in the Promised Land. Describing the woman's mouth, the man says that milk and honey are under her tongue (Song 4:11), and the combination of milk and honey denotes the blessing of the land (Ex 3:8).

Third, Eden and its garden echo in various scenes. The couple is naked and unashamed (Song 1:12-14; 4:1–5:1; 5:10-16; 7:1-9), a state reminiscent of Adam and Eve. The woman is compared to a garden (Song 4:12, 15; 5:1). The woman says, "I am my beloved's and his desire is for me" (Song 7:10), which is the reverse of what God told Eve ("Your desire shall be contrary to your husband," in Gen 3:16).

With language invoking the people and king of Israel, the Promised Land, and the Garden of Eden, the Song of Songs connects us to larger biblical ideas. Rather than seeing the song as unrelated to previous and subsequent Scripture, we should interpret the song as we would other Old Testament books: we should allow the light of the fuller, canonical revelation of Scripture to illuminate what is going on in it. What we see is a king entering into a covenant with his bride, and they dwell in settings that recall the paradise of Eden and the blessings of Canaan.[5]

The language in Isaiah 5 sounds like the kind of thing we would read in Solomon's song. The Lord says, "Let me sing for my beloved my love song concerning his vineyard: My beloved had a vineyard on a very fertile hill. He dug it and cleared it of stones, and planted it with choice vines; he built a watchtower in the midst of it, and hewed out a wine vat in it; and he looked for it to yield grapes, but it yielded wild grapes" (Is 5:1-2). The Lord interprets what the "beloved" and "vineyard" refer to: "For the vineyard of the LORD of hosts is the house of Israel, and the men of Judah are his pleasant planting; and he looked for justice, but behold, bloodshed; for righteousness, but behold, an outcry!" (Is 5:7).

While Isaiah 5:1-7 depicts a vineyard characterized by injustice, the setting in the Song of Songs is pleasant and altogether lovely. Nevertheless, the language in Isaiah 5:1-7 confirms that a song for "my beloved," as well as the presence of a vineyard, has poetic overtones about God's relationship with his people. Seeing these overtones at work in the Song of Songs is intertextually reasonable and is well-established in the history of biblical interpretation. The covenanted couple is typological of Christ and his church. Jesus is the true Son of David, who is greater than Solomon. He is the shepherd-king who seeks his bride and cherishes his vineyard. His voice calls to his church, and he leads his people with steadfast love and unwavering faithfulness.

Discerning the typological truths interwoven in the song will help us grow wise as we interpret it, because just as we need to see the man and woman in light of the Bible's big story, we need to see our own lives in light of the Bible's big story. Wisdom involves delight in covenant relationship. Wisdom involves holy pleasure, deep joy, and the peace of Eden's bygone setting. Wisdom involves longing for what is good and true and beautiful.

---

[5]Hamilton says, "Through the cursed land they travel to gardens, vineyards, and places of springtime fertility, renewing the intimacy of Eden. The joy of verdant fields, flocks, and fellow heirs in the grace of life redounds in the Song to the glory of God. The seed of the woman, son of David, king in Jerusalem, has overcome the curse and taken his loving wife to a lush garden." James M. Hamilton Jr., *God's Glory in Salvation Through Judgment: A Biblical Theology* (Wheaton, IL: Crossway, 2010), 308.

By seeing marriage as a parable, we will more wisely see our earthly marriages as temporal realities that anticipate lasting and more glorious realities. An effect of seeing typological truths in Solomon's song is the stirring of our affections for Godward living and the hope of everlasting life with God. We are a new covenant people, heading toward a new and better Jerusalem, led by a true and greater Solomon. His covenant love is better than anything we find in this world.

LOVE AS STRONG AS DEATH

We are in a new covenant that is more secure than the heavens and the earth. Not even death will separate us from God's love (Rom 8:38-39). The kind of love God has for his people is a covenant love. Though marital love is for this life only, it is a parable of a greater and deeper and lasting love.

Near the end of the Song of Songs, the words of the woman extol love's strength. She says to the man, "Set me as a seal upon your heart, as a seal upon your arm, for love is strong as death, jealousy is fierce as the grave. Its flashes are flashes of fire, the very flame of the LORD" (Song 8:6). A seal is a mark of belonging, of devotion. The seal represents the woman, and she wants the seal on the heart and arm of her beloved. He will carry her with him wherever he goes. There will always be a reminder of his promise and covenant.

The woman compares the strength of love with something else that is notoriously strong. What mortal can withstand the might of Death? No matter how long someone lives, the day of death will come. The grave is "fierce," she says. Just think about a cemetery. Does anything seem as certain in this life as the end of life? Gravestones are markers of triumph over mortal flesh. Like a predator, Death seeks its prey with a fierce determination, and its grip on them seems intractable.

Covenant love is a rival to death. Love's "jealousy" (Song 8:6) is a holy and pure jealousy, the kind that rightly characterizes a covenant union. Love's flashes "are flashes of fire, the very flame of the LORD" (Song 8:6). The imagery may recall Mount Sinai in Exodus 19, where God's holy presence descended in fire and smoke and thunder. The flames of the Lord represented a theophany, which was clear on a smaller scale when Moses saw the flaming bush in

Exodus 3. Mount Sinai was a place of covenant. While at the base of Sinai, the Israelites entered into a covenant with Yahweh (Ex 24). Invoking a covenant context would be appropriate as the woman in the song describes the power and devotion of love.

What if the woman's words present covenant love not only as a rival to death but as a reality even greater than death? She says, "Many waters cannot quench love, neither can floods drown it" (Song 8:7). If the previous verse recalled the theophanic glory of Sinai, the language in this verse may recall the deliverance of the Israelites through the Red Sea. God's people go through the waters. The enemies of God's people were overwhelmed by the waters in Exodus 14. Going all the way back to Genesis 6–8, the many waters of the deluge prevailed over the enemies of God.

In the Old Testament stories, the floodwaters do not conquer God's people. The woman draws on this truth when she emphasizes the greatness of covenant love. Such love is a fierce and holy fire of God that cannot be quenched. You would think that water would prevail over fire, because we have all seen water put out flames. But covenant love is different. Because the earthly marriage of the couple is a parable for the Christ-church union, the holy and unquenchable love in the Song is the divine love that is demonstrated and forever sustained in the new covenant.

Thinking about the unquenchable, unceasing, unwavering love of God toward us will help us grow wise. Sin is destabilizing, and temptations offer us bankrupt promises. We seek stability and security. We are looking for identity and meaning. We are trying to find satisfaction and happiness, but the path of folly is filled with sin's lies and snares. Our souls fret with the spiritual angst and desperation that are part of seeking from the world what can only be found in God.

Meditating on God's steadfast love has a calming effect on anxious hearts. While there may be floods of sorrows threatening to overcome us in this life, the fire of divine love endures. We did nothing to deserve God's love, and we cannot do anything that will undermine it. God's covenant love does not fluctuate. He does not love us more at our best, and he does not love us less at our worst. He loves us in Christ because union with Christ is the reality of the new covenant.

At the end of the prayer in John 17, Jesus says, "I made known to them your name, and I will continue to make it known, that the love with which you have loved me may be in them, and I in them" (Jn 17:26). God loves us with the love that the Son himself has received. Our standing with God could not be more secure. Our future life with God could not be more certain. God's love for us will last for as long as the life he has given us. That life—and thus that love—is *eternal*.

CONCLUSION

After the wisest man who had ever lived wrote the greatest song he had ever composed, interpreters studied its lyrics and sought to discern its meaning and significance. Just as Solomon's proverbs discern and hold forth truth and beauty in the order of God's world, we should expect that Song of Songs points us to wisdom and goodness in God's world. We sense the draw of Eden, the hope of glory, and the beauty of life with God. Solomon's song gives these senses. Since it lifts our gaze in a Godward direction, it leads us in wisdom.

Sin has corrupted loveliness in God's world. Deceit obscures our vision and diminishes the goodness of what he has designed. The Song of Songs stirs our hearts with longings for what this world cannot fulfill. In keeping with the history of Christian interpretation, we should see the song as more than poetic exchanges and encounters between a man and a woman. God created marriage to reflect or shadow greater and lasting realities.

The path of wisdom is a path of life, and Christ the shepherd-king leads us into the eternal peace and joy that only God can give. The Song of Songs is important for our discipleship because we are affected by what we behold. By beholding the glories and delights of communion in the song, we can see that the origin of these things is the unending flame of covenant love in the heart of the triune God.

Chapter Eight

A FLEETING LIFE UNDER THE SUN

THE BOOK OF ECCLESIASTES does not exactly feel like a warm hug. It is more like a splash of cold water to the face. But if you are being lulled to sleep when you need to be alert and sober-minded, a splash of cold water can be a gift, a lifesaver.

If we are going to be wise, we have to welcome uncomfortable truths. We have to be willing to sit with difficult realities, such as unanswered questions, the futility of work, and the inevitability of death. One manifestation of folly is the resistance to dealing with reality. Foolishness does not want to acknowledge the way things are. So, when the writer is helping readers grow wise, he gives a heavy dose of what life is like in a fallen world.

As Charles Dickens writes, "It was the best of times, it was the worst of times, it was the age of wisdom, it was the age of foolishness."[1] Those descriptions capture the complexity of the times.

---

[1] This is the opening to *A Tale of Two Cities* by Charles Dickens, first published in 1859.

CONTENT APPROVED AND ENDORSED

So far I have framed Ecclesiastes as wisdom to embrace. But not every interpreter is so sure that the content of the book can be trusted.[2] The speaker's words are quite grim at times: he claims that animals and people have the same destiny, and he makes comments about how stillborn children are better off than the living. Can the attitude and worldview of the speaker really be trusted?

I think the answer is yes.[3] If we pay attention to structural elements in the book, we will see that Ecclesiastes 1:1-11 forms a prologue to the body of the book, which leads to an epilogue in Ecclesiastes 12:8-14. The opening and closing sections of the book are in the third person, and the body of the work unfolds in the first person.

There is much scholarly discussion about how the opening and closing sections relate to the body of the book. Are they from the same author or from different authors? I do not think we can ultimately be sure whether the frame of the book was provided by an author different from the first-person "Preacher." My inclination is that a second writer provided an introduction and conclusion to the wisdom material. Nevertheless, the resulting words in the book known as Ecclesiastes are inspired by the Holy Spirit, whether the Spirit worked through one human author or through more than one (2 Tim 3:16).

In Ecclesiastes 12:8-14, the book is coming to an end, and in this epilogue we find a strong endorsement of the book's content. In Ecclesiastes 12:9, the writer calls the Preacher "wise" and someone who "taught the people

---

[2] See, e.g., Jerry Shepherd's Ecclesiastes commentary in vol. 6 of *The Expositor's Bible Commentary* (Grand Rapids, MI: Zondervan Academic, 2008).

[3] The writer of Ecclesiastes tells us difficult things, but that does not make those things untrue. His work is not full of contradictions. Instead, he says things requiring reflection—which is what we would expect from a writer of wisdom. In order to understand some of these difficult statements in Ecclesiastes, we need to keep in mind the earthly perspective from which he is saying such things. For example, when he writes, "I thought the dead who are already dead more fortunate than the living who are still alive" (Eccles 4:2), he is not saying that being alive is bad. He is talking about how the dead do not have to experience earthly suffering anymore. Those who are still alive will suffer under the sun, but suffering under the sun has ended for those who have died. When we interpret challenging statements (such as Eccles 4:2) in context, and when we remember the perspective from which the writer is saying them, those statements are less abrasive and more evidently true.

knowledge." So the content between the prologue and epilogue came from a wise person who taught wisdom. This Preacher was not rash or thoughtless with his words, either. Wise people know better than to talk like that. His practice was "weighing and studying and arranging many proverbs with great care" (Eccles 12:9). The frame narrator is telling us that the Preacher's teachings—called "proverbs"—were the result of the Preacher's prolonged reflection and careful construction. Then the writer says, "The Preacher sought to find words of delight, and uprightly he wrote words of truth" (Eccles 12:10). He is evaluating the Preacher's words, which comprise Ecclesiastes 1:12–12:7. They are "words of truth" and not error. He thought about how to write the content, using "words of delight." And he accomplished his task "uprightly." The cumulative effect of Ecclesiastes 12:9-10 is that the writer of the epilogue is issuing a wholehearted endorsement of what we read in the body of Ecclesiastes.[4] The book is biblical wisdom through and through, not a document riddled with errors that must be sifted out.

Having looked at the end of Ecclesiastes, now let's look at the beginning. The Preacher is called "the son of David, king in Jerusalem" (Eccles 1:1). This description is another reason we should receive the content of Ecclesiastes as biblical wisdom that should inform and direct our lives. We have seen similar openings to biblical books:

"The proverbs of Solomon, son of David, king of Israel" (Prov 1:1)

"The Song of Songs, which is Solomon's" (Song 1:1)

The first line in Ecclesiastes has "the son of David, king in Jerusalem" (Eccles 1:1), which is closest to Proverbs 1:1. Since there is no author named at the opening of the book, Ecclesiastes is technically anonymous. But there is not a more likely author for the book's wisdom than Solomon. And if the wisdom in

---

[4]Robertson is right when he says, "In reviewing this concluding evaluation of the work of Qohelet the Convener, we find it difficult to imagine a more appreciative recommendation. Any author receiving an evaluation framed in these words would be compelled to respond with embarrassment and humble appreciation. In light of this extensive commendation of the body of the book as found in the epilogue, it would indeed be difficult to support the idea of two conflicting messages in the one book of Ecclesiastes. If there are two authors, they are in total agreement." O. Palmer Robertson, *The Christ of Wisdom: A Redemptive-Historical Exploration of the Wisdom Books of the Old Testament* (Phillipsburg, NJ: P&R, 2017), 243.

Ecclesiastes is Solomonic, that fact bolsters even more our confidence in taking the content of the book as wisdom to embrace and apply.

Ecclesiastes 1:12 tells us the Preacher was king over Israel in Jerusalem, and this geographical situation would not have lasted beyond his son Rehoboam, because Rehoboam provoked a rebellion that divided the united kingdom in 930 BC. Solomon was the last king whose entire reign was over the whole land and based in the capital, Jerusalem. Solomon certainly fits the "son of David" description in Ecclesiastes 1:1. And the vast wealth and flocks and concubines (Eccles 2:4-8) fit with Solomon's reign as well. The Preacher says he "surpassed all who were before me in Jerusalem. Also my wisdom remained with me" (Eccles 2:9). Solomon's greatness and wisdom surpassed those who preceded him. Furthermore, Ecclesiastes 5:1 refers to "the house of God," which denotes the Jerusalem temple. The temple was built during Solomon's reign.

The previous considerations support a Solomonic origin of the book's wisdom. Even if a separate writer introduced and ended the book, we can reasonably attribute the wisdom of Ecclesiastes to King Solomon, the son of David who ruled from Jerusalem over all Israel. No wonder, then, that the epilogue positively evaluates and endorses the content of the book. The writer would be the nation's shepherd-king, whose wisdom surpassed any who had ever lived. His writings could be trusted. In the subsequent arguments in this chapter, I will be assuming the Solomonic source of the wisdom in Ecclesiastes and its total trustworthiness regarding whichever subject the writer addresses.

DAYS LIKE A VAPOR

The second verse of the book is bracing: "Vanity of vanities, says the Preacher, vanity of vanities! All is vanity" (Eccles 1:2). The Hebrew word (*hebel*) is about what is vaporous and fleeting. So when the Preacher says everything is vanity, he is speaking from a perspective larger than this earthly life. In an ultimate sense, what we do seems vain because life does not last. However, the writer is not saying that life is meaningless. I prefer to translate the end of Ecclesiastes 1:2 as "Everything is vaporous" or "Everything is fleeting." The transience of life is the point. And because of the transience of life, frustrations abound.[5] Frustrating, frustrating, everything is frustrating! Can you not sense how nothing lasts? No matter how hard we work, death will come. No matter how many friends we make, death will come. No matter how wise or righteous we are, death will come. Life is fleeting, vaporous, like a breath. This truth is the point in James's letter where he says, "What is your life? For you are a mist that appears for a little time and then vanishes" (Jas 4:14). Why does James write in such a way about the brevity of life? Because he believes one of the key themes in Ecclesiastes.

Apparently, a key to wisdom is remembering you will die.[6] Does that seem morbid? The writer is not recommending that we obsess over our future death. But when we remember that we are not invincible and that we are more vulnerable than we realize, there is a resulting insight and growth that the righteous experience.

The rhythms of the world can increase our perspective about our relative importance. Generations come and go, but the earth continues on (Eccles 1:4). The sun rises and sets, the wind blows and makes its rounds, and the streams return to the sea (Eccles 1:5-7). Amid these rhythms, we are born and then we die. Sobering, right? That is the point. Wisdom is not found in self-exaltation or self-importance. The wind was blowing before we were born, and the sun will be shining after we are gone. The opening prologue of Ecclesiastes will disabuse us of the notion that the world revolves around us.

A worker will toil and toil, but what will happen to the fruit of labor? The writer says, "I must leave it to the man who will come after me, and who knows whether he will be wise or a fool? Yet he will be master of all for which I toiled and used my wisdom under the sun. This also is vanity" (Eccles 2:18-19). There is an agony on display here. We cannot ultimately control our lives or what happens after we die. The fruit of our labor may be received by a wise

---

[5]Robertson suggests that "frustration of frustrations" is a good way to translate Eccles 1:2. He says, "If 'transitoriness' or 'vanity' may be viewed as representing the objective side of the word *hebel*, 'frustration' best represents the effect of this transitoriness or vanity on the human psyche. A human being's normal reaction to the fleeting character of every experience in life is a sense of frustration" (*Christ of Wisdom*, 251).
[6]For an insightful treatment of this notion, see Matthew McCullough, *Remember Death: The Surprising Path to Living Hope* (Wheaton, IL: Crossway, 2018).

person who will steward it well, or maybe a fool will take over what we have done and ruin it all. We cannot control the results of our toil.

There is no ultimate security in this world. The writer asks, "What has a man from all the toil and striving of heart with which he toils beneath the sun?" (Eccles 2:22). In one sense, we can answer "income" or "a house" or "food for myself and others." Those are all things we can gain from toil. But the writer would know all of that already. His question is not about temporal gain. He is asking about what, in the big picture, we gain from our toil.

All our labor will still lead to our death. The writer emphasizes this point because he discerns that we live in a Genesis 3 world. God told Adam, "Cursed is the ground because of you; in pain you shall eat of it all the days of your life" (Gen 3:17), and, "By the sweat of your face you shall eat bread, till you return to the ground, for out of it you were taken; for you are dust, and to dust you shall return" (Gen 3:19). God's words to Adam are a promise of toilsome work, and the writer of Ecclesiastes notes the fulfillment of it.

The writer alludes to Genesis 3:19 when he says, "All go to one place. All are from the dust, and to dust all return" (Eccles 3:20). This claim is not a denial of the afterlife. It is spoken from an earthly perspective. Everyone goes to the grave. "The wise person has his eyes in his head, but the fool walks in darkness. And yet I perceived that the same event happens to all of them" (Eccles 2:14). This "same event" is death. Because earthly life is fleeting, the breath of life will someday expire for us all. There is a time to be born and a time to die (Eccles 3:1).

BEYOND TRACING OUT

Everything that takes place on earth is "under the sun" (Eccles 1:3) and "under heaven" (Eccles 3:1). But there is a God who rules above the sun and over the heavens and the earth. He is sovereign and supreme in the world he has made. He has appointed the times and the seasons.

The writer of Ecclesiastes says, "For everything there is a season, and a time for every matter under heaven" (Eccles 3:1). Events in this world do not occur randomly. We do not live in a universe originating from or sustained by chance. The writer mentions killing and healing, weeping and laughing, seeking and losing, war and peace. All the happenings of life are subsumed under the pairs of terms in Ecclesiastes 3:1-8.

While life is taking place around us, we want to discern what God is doing in the world and why things happen the way they do (Eccles 3:11). This impulse is understandable, though it is ultimately in vain. We cannot trace out the ways of God because we do not have the mind of God. "For who has known the mind of the Lord, or who has been his counselor?" (Rom 11:34). The depths of God's riches are unreachable, his judgments are unsearchable, and his ways are inscrutable (Rom 11:33).

We must understand that there are countless things we will not understand. Herein is wisdom. The writer of Ecclesiastes says, "Consider the work of God: who can make straight what he has made crooked? In the day of prosperity be joyful, and in the day of disaster consider: God has made the one as well as the other, so that man may not find out anything that will be after him" (Eccles 7:13-14). We cannot fully control, nor can we fully understand, what happens in our lives or in the lives of others.

Think of the questions people ask about many different situations. Why did this person get cancer? Why did that person lose her job? How did the marriage fail? Why did that child die? How could that person abandon the faith he professed? Where should she apply even when employers keep rejecting her application? How could this person abuse that child? Why is he deployed for so long and so far away? Will we ever feel happy again? Will we ever be financially stable? Is this depression my new normal? Why will my spouse not open up to me? Why did that person get the opportunity I wanted?

There is so much we do not know and will not know. Are we okay with that? Have we resolved that the Lord is wise and trustworthy in his governance of the world? Living wisely in our humanity will mean embracing the limits of what it means to be human. And we lack comprehensive knowledge of what happens in the world and why. Try as we might, "man cannot find out the work that is done under the sun. However much man may toil in seeking, he will not find it out. Even though a wise man claims to know, he cannot find it out" (Eccles 8:17). Do we believe Solomon's wisdom here? Are we prepared to abandon the pursuit of omniscience?

We are called to worship God without trying to be God. Seeking the knowledge that belongs only to God is like trying to shepherd the wind. The wind is ungraspable. We cannot grab the wind in order to steer it. We cannot control life and demand that it go in the direction we prefer. We need to cheerfully submit to the reality of God's sovereignty and our non-sovereignty. We need to pray for the humility to breathe in and rest in the good news that "for those who love God all things work together for good, for those who are called according to his purpose" (Rom 8:28).

The combination of divine sovereignty and divine goodness is great news for God's people. When we feel like things are beyond our control, we might feel paralyzed with fear or deeply worried about the present and future. Since the biblical authors do not entertain any delusions that we can control our lives or shepherd the wind, we face the responsibility to receive the truth of what it means for God to be God.

FOOD AND DRINK AND TOIL—AND JOY

Though God does not promise to fill our minds with the answers and explanations of what happens in the world he has made, he will grant us what we need to live faithfully in this world for his glory. Several passages in Ecclesiastes highlight the theme of joy from God's hand, and we need to see that this gift is vital for a wise life under the sun.

The writer says,

> There is nothing better for a person than that he should eat and drink and find enjoyment in his toil. This also, I saw, is from the hand of God, for apart from him who can eat or who can have enjoyment? For the one who pleases him God has given wisdom and knowledge and joy, but to the sinner he has given the business of gathering and collecting, only to give to one who pleases God. (Eccles 2:24-26)

Another passage where these notions appear is in Ecclesiastes 3: "I perceived that there is nothing better for them than to be joyful and to do good as long as they live; also that everyone should eat and drink and take pleasure in his toil—this is God's gift to man" (Eccles 3:12-13).

In these two passages from Ecclesiastes 2–3, the focus is on frequent—even daily—activities. People regularly eat, drink, and work, and the frequency is the point. What we do regularly can become mundane. Work is not always exciting, and most of the time eating and drinking does not feel like a party. In fact, most of what we do every day involves routine. Sure, there is some variation, but eating and drinking and toiling can seem part of our day-to-day lives.

The writer of Ecclesiastes wants us to have joy in the small things, not just joy in the big things. When we think of big events, such as weddings or birthdays or anniversaries or graduations, we know that joy is naturally associated with them. Big moments warrant pictures, and they are the kind of things that show up on social media.

But what if we can have joy in daily food and drink and toil? What if there is a genuine satisfaction in God's gifts to us? Not a satisfaction that is idolatrous or unseemly, but a satisfaction rooted in gratitude to God and in the faithful stewardship of what God has allotted us. Paul sounds like the writer of Ecclesiastes when he says, "So, whether you eat or drink, or whatever you do, do all to the glory of God" (1 Cor 10:31).

Life is in the details, right? That means the seemingly mundane things of life can become catalysts for thanksgiving and praise. God's will for us is that we rejoice always, pray without ceasing, and give thanks in all circumstances (1 Thess 5:16-18).

Think about work. Not all jobs are a pleasure ride. But when we apply ourselves to work with integrity and discipline, and then from that work we earn income for our lives and for others who are depending on us, there is something deeply gratifying about fulfilling our responsibilities. So the Preacher says, "Whatever your hand finds to do, do it with your might" (Eccles 9:10).

As we thank God for food and drink, and as we seek to glorify him in faithful work, we need to be prayerful that money not subtly become our god and reason for living. The Preacher warns us about this: "He who loves money will not be satisfied with money, nor he who loves wealth with his income; this also is vanity" (Eccles 5:10). Those who make earning money the reason for life will not be satisfied with a certain amount. They have fallen prey to the voice of Lady Folly, who whispers to them that worldly riches and possessions will satisfy their hearts.

Riches are unstable and therefore are a terrible object of hope (Eccles 5:13-15). Paul says,

> If we have food and clothing, with these we will be content. But those who desire to be rich fall into temptation, into a snare, into many senseless and harmful desires that plunge people into ruin and destruction. For the love of money is a root of all kinds of evils. It is through this craving that some have wandered away from the faith and pierced themselves with many pangs. (1 Tim 6:8-10)

We need to walk in such gratitude to God that contentment does not seem crazy to our minds and that money always seems unworthy of our devotion. Receiving, from God's hand, the gift of joy in our food and drink and toil will mean at the same time refusing to serve money. "No one can serve two masters," Jesus says, "for either he will hate the one and love the other, or he will be devoted to the one and despise the other. You cannot serve God and money" (Mt 6:24).

Instead of seeking wealth, we should seek the kingdom of God. Jesus says, "Seek first the kingdom of God and his righteousness, and all these things will be added to you" (Mt 6:33). We should work hard, trust God's provision, receive his blessings with gratitude and contentment, and devote our hearts to the reality of his everlasting kingdom.

No matter how long we live, our life is just a few days in the grand scheme of things. "Behold, what I have seen to be good and fitting is to eat and drink and find enjoyment in all the toil with which one toils under the sun the few days of his life that God has given him, for this is his lot" (Eccles 5:18). Does God want you to be joyful in this life? Yes, for that is what his Word teaches. The Preacher says, "I commend joy, for man has nothing better under the sun but to eat and drink and be joyful, for this will go with him in his toil through the days of his life that God has given him under the sun" (Eccles 8:15).

The Preacher is telling us what is *better*. In fact, he does that a lot in Ecclesiastes.

KNOWING WHAT IS BETTER

The words of the Preacher not only point us to wisdom, but his words identify what the "better" choice in different situations can be. Sometimes the wisdom passages of Scripture instruct us on what is clearly right and clearly wrong. But growth in wisdom involves discerning what is "better," since not all options in life necessarily carry a moral value.

What if you are in the situation of having to decide whether to attend a lunch party or a funeral? All things being equal, neither option is obviously right or wrong. But the writer of Ecclesiastes says, "It is better to go to the house of mourning than to go to the house of feasting, for this is the end of all mankind, and the living will lay it to heart" (Eccles 7:2). He says the better choice, then, would be attending the funeral, because the increase of our sober-mindedness about our lives is a good thing. Funerals remind us that we are not invincible, that death is our future, and that we may be dead sooner than we think.

Is it wrong to attend the house of feasting? Not at all! We have memories of joyful meals and celebrations so wonderful that we did not want them to end. We should welcome times in a house of feasting, and we should endeavor to make our home such a place for others to feast and celebrate.

But according to the Preacher, when we are faced with attending either the house of mourning or the house of feasting, the house of mourning is the *better* choice because of the sheer weight of truth that our hearts confront there. The living "will lay it to heart," meaning that those who attend funerals should be wiser as a result of reflecting on death. Those in the house of mourning are coming face to face with the reality of their own mortality. They are reminded that death "is the end of all mankind" (Eccles 7:2).

Discerning what is better in certain circumstances may not be easy or clear cut, and the same choice might not work for every person. But growth in wisdom will mean incorporating factors into our decision making that go beyond what may be obviously right or wrong. If God has forbidden something, let us not seek to justify it. If God has allowed something, let us not prohibit it. But in nonmoral matters, wisdom will mean discerning what is better for you in particular.

Several questions can help us think through what is better. We can consider the costs of time and resources. We can ponder the effects on ourselves or others. We can ask questions about our witness for Christ and our reputation as a Christian. We can think through whether the disadvantages will outnumber the advantages. We can welcome the counsel of others as we weigh options. We can wonder about risk or opportunity or timing. These are the kinds of factors that we should consider in order to discern what the better choice will be.

Wisdom means knowing that, in the end, God will use even our unwise choices to form us, sanctify us, and teach us. We should not be paralyzed in decision making. We need to prayerfully make the best decision we can, with the given factors we can identify, and then leave the results to the Lord.

The Preacher says, "He who observes the wind will not sow, and he who regards the clouds will not reap" (Eccles 11:4). If the time for sowing has arrived, the sower must not make excuses. If the time for reaping has come, the clouds should not be the reason not to harvest. If we search hard enough and long enough, we can always come up with a reason not to do the things we are supposed to do. As we are faced with various decisions in life, we should not let the "wind" or the "clouds" keep us from acting. The inability to make decisions is rooted in fear—a fear that we will choose the wrong thing or that we will not be able to control what happens next.

But the good news is that God is sovereign and fully trustworthy. And sometimes the way we make better decisions is through the hard lessons learned when we made poorer ones. If we are faced with various job choices, potential mates, different places we could live, or several colleges we could attend, we do not need to buckle under the pressures. We can remember that God is faithful, be prayerful as we consider factors that are at play, invite the wisdom of trusted counselors, and then . . . make a decision, trusting God with the results.

WISER IN COMMUNITY

To make decisions and to grow wise ourselves, we need to walk with the wise. The Preacher says,

> Two are better than one, because they have a good reward for their toil. For if they fall, one will lift up his fellow. But woe to him who is alone when he falls and has not another to lift him up! Again, if two lie together, they keep warm, but how can one keep warm alone? And though a man might prevail

against one who is alone, two will withstand him—a threefold cord is not quickly broken. (Eccles 4:9-12)

We will not do well without friends.[7] And we will not grow wise without wise friends. The Lord has designed his image bearers to be communal creatures. Despite any personality proclivities we may have, we need healthy relationships. In order to thrive spiritually, we should pursue and cultivate friendships with those who fear the Lord. These individuals may be older, younger, or the same age we are.

The important thing is that we not entangle our lives with fools, because we will be influenced by those with whom we share significant time and experiences. The Preacher says, "It is better for a man to hear the rebuke of the wise than to hear the song of fools" (Eccles 7:5). The "song of fools" is probably what would take place in a festive gathering where the focus is levity and indulgence. You can imagine a scene where people, already impaired by their wine, lift their cups with shallow tunes that distract from the more important things of life. The song of fools may even have a good beat and memorable lyrics, but if the message is folly, then the song is not aiming at our deepest good.

A song, however, is more pleasant than a rebuke. The Preacher knew this, which is why he constructed his wise saying the way he did. We naturally incline toward what feels—or sounds—better in the moment. We naturally recoil from what is unpleasant or humiliating. But what our hearts most deeply need is not necessarily what will be pleasant in the short term. A rebuke from a wise person will do us more good, in both the short term and the long term, than the song of fools.

If we are going to receive the rebuke of the wise, we must be in community with the wise. The proverb is true: "Whoever walks with the wise becomes wise, but the companion of fools will suffer harm" (Prov 13:20). The Preacher in Ecclesiastes believes this truth. Though it may be elegantly performed and publicly lauded, the song of fools will not bless the listener or help the listener walk the path of wisdom—other than the song revealing what not to believe or do.

---

[7] For a book-length reflection on friendship, see Drew Hunter, *Made for Friendship: The Relationship That Halves Our Sorrows and Doubles Our Joys* (Wheaton, IL: Crossway, 2018).

The Preacher's wisdom in Ecclesiastes 7:5 does not mean the wise lack songs. The very existence of the Psalms, for instance, is evidence for a melody in the heart and mouth of those who fear the Lord. What the Preacher pushes against is the song of fools. Better than such songs is the rebuke of the wise, even though the rebuke is initially uncomfortable for the one who receives it. If an unpleasant rebuke is received, and is the catalyst for correction and wiser choices, then the soul is strengthened under the sun.

We need the community of the wise to remind us that life is not frivolous. Life matters, people matter, our choices matter, and most of all, eternal things matter. The wise want their lives as well as their songs shaped by the purpose for which God made us.

THE WHOLE DUTY OF HUMANKIND

The final words of Ecclesiastes summarize not only the book itself; they also summarize the responsibilities of God's image bearers. The writer says, "The end of the matter; all has been heard. Fear God and keep his commandments, for this is the whole duty of man. For God will bring every deed into judgment, with every secret thing, whether good or evil" (Eccles 12:13-14).

The manifestation of fearing God is obeying God, which is why the writer says that humanity's "whole duty" is to "fear God" and "keep his commandments." This whole-life reverence is what matters most, because it is informed by eternal truths. It is more valuable than earthly fame and riches. It is more lasting than earthly toil and accomplishments. It is more fulfilling than earthly pleasures and pursuits.

Our duty is that for which we *exist*. We exist to know God, to worship God, to delight in God. Such a reverential response to God's revelation is denoted by "fearing God" and "keeping his commandments." This present responsibility (in Eccles 12:13) is explained with a view toward the future (in Eccles 12:14, the next verse). God will "bring every deed into judgment." There is a God, and he is the righteous judge of all. Our actions matter because the end of this life is not the end of all things.

The writer of Ecclesiastes looks toward future realities. The end of the book points to a future judgment, but it merely reinforces what earlier verses have claimed. In Ecclesiastes 3:17, the Preacher is comforted in the face of injustice when he remembers, "God will judge the righteous and the wicked, for there is a time for every matter and for every work." Though there are present examples of the wicked prospering and the righteous not thriving, "it will be well with those who fear God, because they fear before him" (Eccles 8:12). The future and final judgment of God will have the last word, and that promise is good news for God's people.

Promises about the future should shape the way people live here and now. The Preacher wants his audience to fear the Lord. Though the book ends on that note (Eccles 12:13-14), he speaks about that notion earlier. Being aware of the supreme and unassailable sovereignty of God over all things, people should fear the Lord (Eccles 3:14). Fearing God is the best thing we can do in light of what God has revealed about himself (Eccles 7:18; 8:12).

Fearing the Lord should take place as early as possible. The writer exhorts the young to walk wisely and remember the Creator (Eccles 11:9; 12:1). Like the book of Proverbs, Ecclesiastes envisions its primary audience as youth who have a long life before them on the path of wisdom. The aged are not exempt from the book's wisdom, of course, yet the Preacher speaks as an older man to those younger. He has seen the many griefs and wrong turns that take place under the sun, and now he appeals to those who look at the horizon of life before them and have many choices to make.

Life is short, so they need to remember the inevitability of death and the future judgment. This perspective is necessary for true wisdom, that they might fear the Lord and turn from evil.

CONCLUSION

Ecclesiastes confronts the reader with uncomfortable truths that are foundational for a wise life. Whether we live twenty or fifty or ninety years on this earth, life is but a breath, a vapor. During the days the Lord has allotted for us, we face inscrutable and sorrowful things, and we become aware of suffering in the lives of those around us and around the world. We realize that life is not getting easier as we get older.

But in the midst of a Genesis 3 world, there is joy from the hand of God as we live, move, and have our being. Though toilsome, work is a gift. Though fleeting, the earthly blessings of God are meaningful and must be stewarded faithfully by his image bearers. The fleeting nature of earthly pleasures corresponds to the nature of our bodies and earthly life: under the sun, we are fleeting. There is a time to be born and a time to die, and the one who has appointed these times is the all-sovereign and ever-wise God.

The main burden of Ecclesiastes is to help us live with sober-mindedness throughout our earthly pilgrimage, and the writer accomplishes this goal by framing present responsibilities in light of larger and lasting truths. The promise of a future judgment should affect how and why we make the choices we do. Our march toward the grave should give us humility before the God who has numbered our days.

Chapter Nine

FOLLOWING LADY FOLLY INTO EXILE

WE CAN IMAGINE THE HEARTBREAK of wise parents who see their child wander from truth and plunge headlong into the depths of folly. We can imagine a church's sorrow at seeing beloved members forsake the way of Christ and pursue a path of rebellion. Can we imagine this tragedy on a national level?

What would it look like for an entire nation to hear the voice of Lady Folly and follow her lead? What would be the result of such stubbornness and foolishness? Where would Lady Folly take her disciples?

Lady Folly leads her followers into captivity, exile, and death. And that is the path the people of Israel walked in the Old Testament story line. Of course, Lady Folly never tells us ahead of time that she is leading us toward disaster. She is far too deceptive, far too subtle, for that kind of straight talk.

SOLOMON'S TURN TOWARD FOLLY

Given what we know of Solomon's great wisdom in 1 Kings 3–10, we might find the final part of his life rather jolting. But there are clues along the way that things are going awry. Remember the expectations for Israel's king in

Deuteronomy 17: "Only he must not acquire many horses for himself or cause the people to return to Egypt in order to acquire many horses, since the LORD has said to you, 'You shall never return that way again.' And he shall not acquire many wives for himself, lest his heart turn away, nor shall he acquire for himself excessive silver and gold" (Deut 17:16-17).

In 1 Kings, the biblical author narrates Solomon's violation of these expectations. Solomon acquires excessive wealth (1 Kings 10:14-29), and he gathers together many thousands of chariots and horsemen (1 Kings 10:26-27). In fact, "Solomon's import of horses was from Egypt and Kue, and the king's traders received them from Kue at a price" (1 Kings 10:28). Not only does Solomon acquire many horses, but he has horses brought specifically *from Egypt*. Then the author says, "King Solomon loved many foreign women, along with the daughter of Pharaoh: Moabite, Ammonite, Edomite, Sidonian, and Hittite women, from the nations concerning which the LORD had said to the people of Israel, 'You shall not enter into marriage with them, neither shall they with you, for surely they will turn away your heart after their gods'" (1 Kings 11:1-2). Solomon has seven hundred wives and three hundred concubines (1 Kings 11:3).

The description of Solomon's situation not only reminds us of Deuteronomy 17, but it corresponds to each element in that earlier chapter, so that we see Solomon's thorough departure from God's expectations for Israel's king. Stephen Dempster says, "As for following Deuteronomy's positive commandments to write out a copy of the Torah and to read it every day, one can assume from his behavior that such practices were nonexistent."[1] As a new Adam, Solomon falls. His "heart was not wholly true to the LORD his God, as was the heart of David his father" (1 Kings 11:4). He is a son of David who does not remain steadfast in true worship and obedience. He "did what was evil in the sight of the LORD" (1 Kings 11:6), evil that included false worship (1 Kings 11:5, 7).

Solomon's departure angers the Lord (1 Kings 11:9). Turning from the Lord, Solomon pursues what is foolish. Though Israel's king is supposed to "learn to fear the LORD his God by keeping all the words of this law" and to "not

---

[1]Stephen G. Dempster, *The Return of the Kingdom: A Biblical Theology of God's Reign*, Essential Studies in Biblical Theology (Downers Grove, IL: IVP Academic, 2024), 125.

turn aside from the commandment, either to the right hand or to the left" (Deut 17:19-20), Solomon "did not keep what the LORD commanded" (1 Kings 11:10), for he "turned away his heart" to idols (1 Kings 11:3-4).

During Solomon's decline, the Lord promises that the kingdom will be torn from Solomon's son (1 Kings 11:11-13). A prophetic action points to what will come. The prophet Ahijah tears a garment into twelve pieces and tells a man named Jeroboam, "Take for yourself ten pieces, for thus says the LORD, the God of Israel, 'Behold, I am about to tear the kingdom from the hand of Solomon and will give you ten tribes'" (1 Kings 11:31).

A KINGDOM TORN ASUNDER

The prophet Ahijah's words are fulfilled during the reign of Solomon's son Rehoboam. The tearing of the kingdom is the result of some foolish decisions. Folly is a corrosive acid on what is good and beautiful. It distorts and destroys. It undermines and humiliates. It allures with false promises and then pounces like a predator.

An assembly of Israelites tells King Rehoboam, "Your father made our yoke heavy. Now therefore lighten the hard service of your father and his heavy yoke on us, and we will serve you" (1 Kings 12:4). Rehoboam takes counsel with old men who had served with his father, Solomon, and they tell him to speak good words to the assembly. But Rehoboam "abandoned the counsel that the old men gave him and took counsel with the young men who had grown up with him and stood before him" (1 Kings 12:8). These young men advise harshness (1 Kings 12:10-11), and Rehoboam follows their words (1 Kings 12:13-14).

When we read about Rehoboam's decision, we can anticipate disaster. We imagine the older counselors to be wiser than the younger advisers, yet the king goes with the younger. He rejects wise counsel and follows the words of young and inexperienced people. The land divides, and tribes in the northern part of Israel make Jeroboam king, while Rehoboam rules in the south (1 Kings 12:16-20).

The united kingdom's division was one of the most consequential events in Israel's history. From that point, the respective kingdoms (northern and southern) would continue until foreign adversaries destroyed them. Stories throughout the rest of 1–2 Kings report the widespread idolatry and rebellion present in the land and exemplified by the rulers. The majority of the Southern Kingdom kings were unrighteous, and all the rulers in the Northern Kingdom were unrighteous. Significantly, no biblical author calls any king after Solomon wise.

The state of Judah during Rehoboam's reign is outrageous:

> And Judah did what was evil in the sight of the LORD, and they provoked him to jealousy with their sins that they committed, more than all that their fathers had done. For they also built for themselves high places and pillars and Asherim on every high hill and under every green tree, and there were also male cult prostitutes in the land. They did according to all the abominations of the nations that the LORD drove out before the people of Israel. (1 Kings 14:22-24)

Though the Southern Kingdom contains the capital (Jerusalem) and thus the temple that was built there during Solomon's reign, the inhabitants nevertheless build idol shrines and engage in sexual immorality along with their false worship. The Israelites live like the pagan Canaanites whom the Lord drove out during the conquest. Their abominations are evidence of departure from God's Word and wisdom.

The Proverbs of Solomon are a fascinating lens through which to see Solomon and his son Rehoboam. As Israel's shepherd-king and the father of the future king, Solomon instructed his son in wisdom and warned against the voice of Lady Folly. Yet when Rehoboam grew up, he did not embody biblical wisdom. His actions were the fruit of a rebellious heart, and his foolishness had nationwide and long-term consequences.

The Northern Kingdom fell to the Assyrians in 722 BC, and 2 Kings 17 gives the theological justification for it. The biblical author says,

> This occurred because the people of Israel had sinned against the LORD their God, who had brought them up out of the land of Egypt from under the hand of Pharaoh king of Egypt, and had feared other gods and walked in the customs of the nations whom the LORD drove out before the people of Israel, and in the customs that the kings of Israel had practiced. And the people of Israel did secretly against the LORD their God things that were not right. (2 Kings 17:7-9)

God raised up prophets who warned the Israelites about their stubbornness and foolishness. The prophets and seers told them the divine plea: "Turn from your evil ways and keep my commandments and my statutes, in accordance with all the Law that I commanded your fathers, and that I sent to you by my servants the prophets" (2 Kings 17:13). Repentance would have been evidence of wisdom, but instead, the nation's stubbornness is evidence of folly.

The Southern Kingdom does not walk in Yahweh's ways either. Even though there are several righteous kings, such as Hezekiah and Josiah, the people's march toward judgment is undeterred. The Southern Kingdom finally falls to Babylon in 586 BC. The Lord said, "I will remove Judah also out of my sight, as I have removed Israel, and I will cast off this city that I have chosen, Jerusalem, and the house of which I said, My name shall be there" (2 Kings 23:27).

The fall of Jerusalem to Babylon and the subsequent Babylonian exile are expressions of divine judgment that Moses foretold in the Torah. If the Israelites rejected Yahweh's commandments, they would "be plucked off the land that you are entering to take possession of it. And the LORD will scatter you among all peoples, from one end of the earth to the other, and there you shall serve other gods of wood and stone, which neither you nor your fathers have known" (Deut 28:63-64). When Babylon conquers the Southern Kingdom and destroys Jerusalem and exiled the people, covenant curses are being fulfilled.

Israel, Yahweh's covenant son (Ex 4:22), rejected his Father's commands and followed the path of folly where it leads: captivity and death. The Babylonian exile is Yahweh's covenant discipline of his covenant son.

A WISE PROPHET IN BABYLON

Not all exiled Israelites are rebellious. In the stages of opposition that lead to Jerusalem's downfall, King Nebuchadnezzar of Babylon deports Israelites who meet certain criteria (Dan 1:3-4). One of the youths is Daniel, and the book that bears his name tells various stories and visions that were part of his time in exile.

Though removed from his homeland, Daniel serves Yahweh in Babylon. His allegiance is uncorrupted (Dan 1:8), and the Lord honors his faithfulness by blessing him with much learning and skill and wisdom (Dan 1:17). In fact,

Daniel and his three Hebrew friends (Shadrach, Meshach, and Abednego) are wiser than anyone else who was tested to serve in the king's administration (Dan 1:19-20).

God raised up prophets before Nebuchadnezzar came along (such as Isaiah, Micah, and Habakkuk), but Daniel is a prophet *in exile*. Daniel is an example of a son who grows up to embrace what his father and mother taught him (Prov 3:1-8). He loves the voice of Lady Wisdom, and he refuses to turn from the law of God.

The king's administration has many magicians, enchanters, sorcerers, and allegedly wise men whom the king relies on, especially when a troubling dream needs an interpretation (Dan 2:1-2). But the king's pagan courtiers are not wise in the ways that matter, and their ignorance reveals their impotence (Dan 2:7-11). When they fail to tell and then interpret Nebuchadnezzar's dream, the lives of all the wise men are under the sentence of death.

Only Daniel can do what they failed to do, and his ability is the gift of the God of heaven. He prays to God, and God answers his prayer. Daniel praises the Lord by describing God as the source of all true knowledge and wisdom:

> Blessed be the name of God forever and ever,
> > to whom belong wisdom and might.
> He changes times and seasons;
> > he removes kings and sets up kings;
> he gives wisdom to the wise
> > and knowledge to those who have understanding;
> he reveals deep and hidden things;
> > he knows what is in the darkness,
> > and the light dwells with him.
> To you, O God of my fathers,
> > I give thanks and praise,
> for you have given me wisdom and might,
> > and have now made known to me what we asked of you,
> > for you have made known to us the king's matter. (Dan 2:20-23)

God revealed to Daniel what was "deep" and "hidden," terms that are about the future. Humankind cannot know the future, though God can disclose any aspects of his plans as he pleases. He was pleased to reveal to Daniel things that were to come. And now wise Daniel is wiser still, possessing understanding about what God disclosed. God has all and perfect wisdom, and thus he knows what cannot be seen and known by mere humanity.

Quickly gaining an audience with Nebuchadnezzar, Daniel reveals the content of the king's dream and its interpretation (Dan 2:31-45). The king's response is an acknowledgment of Daniel's accuracy (Dan 2:46-49). The king makes Daniel "ruler over the whole province of Babylon and chief prefect over all the wise men of Babylon" (Dan 2:48). Daniel is over everyone but the king himself.

A cluster of truths connects Daniel to an earlier Old Testament character. He lived outside the Promised Land, stories tell of his refusal to compromise his character and his obedience to Yahweh, he interpreted the dreams and visions of a ruler, the Lord vindicated him despite false accusations and plots against him, and he was elevated over everyone except the ruler himself. The stories about Daniel are reminiscent of Joseph in Genesis 37–50.

Like Joseph, Daniel is a wise ruler whose wisdom is a blessing to those under his influence and authority. Nebuchadnezzar tells Daniel that "the spirit of the holy gods is in you" (Dan 4:18). This claim is like Pharaoh's comment about Joseph, "Can we find a man like this, in whom is the Spirit of God?" (Gen 41:38). The wisdom and discernment of Joseph and Daniel are not natural but God-given and Spirit-empowered.

As a wise prophet, Daniel warns Nebuchadnezzar about the king's unrighteousness and the threat of divine judgment: "Therefore, O king, let my counsel be acceptable to you: break off your sins by practicing righteousness, and your iniquities by showing mercy to the oppressed, that there may perhaps be a lengthening of your prosperity" (Dan 4:27). Though Daniel is a wise prophet, Nebuchadnezzar is not a wise king. He flaunts his riches and boasts in his greatness, as if all his might were his own doing (Dan 4:29-30). He learns that God's "works are right and his ways are just; and those who walk in pride he is able to humble" (Dan 4:37).

The book of Daniel associates pride with folly, as well as humility with wisdom. Nebuchadnezzar embodies the former pair, and Daniel the latter.

THOSE WHO DESPISE THE WISE

In due course, the Babylonian Empire falls to the Persians. When we enter the narrative in Daniel 6, we are seeing the setup of a new administration over what formerly belonged to Babylon. During this setup, the prophet Daniel experiences a truth as old as Cain and Abel: walking wisely with God will not guarantee favor with others. It might provoke resentment, jealousy, and opposition. The wise accept those outcomes as possible and bearable.

King Darius plans to set Daniel over the whole kingdom (Dan 6:3), so "the high officials and the satraps sought to find a ground of complaint against Daniel with regard to the kingdom, but they could find no ground for complaint or any fault, because he was faithful, and no error or fault was found in him" (Dan 6:4). Another way to understand this description of Daniel is that he walks wisely, so no valid accusation of folly can be made against him.

These men despise Daniel so much, however, that they plan to use his spiritual devotion against him (Dan 6:5). They concoct a plan for the king to sign an injunction that people should pray only to the king for thirty days, and any violators of the injunction will die in a den of lions (Dan 6:7-9). Daniel knows about the document, but he continues his devotion to Yahweh anyway (Dan 6:10). That is what the wise do. They remain steadfast in their allegiance to Yahweh, and they trust him with the results.

When the king reluctantly orders that Daniel be cast into the den of lions, he tells Daniel, "May your God, whom you serve continually, deliver you!" (Dan 6:16). And the next day, Daniel is taken from the den, alive (Dan 6:20-22). God vindicates his faithful servant. Though the conspirators used Daniel's devotion against him and counted on Daniel's death inside that den, the Lord preserved his prophet and servant.

Shadrach, Meshach, and Abednego found themselves in a life-or-death situation earlier in the book. When Nebuchadnezzar ordered the citizens to worship an image, the three Hebrews refused to bow. They knew that idolatry was sinful and dishonorable. Their devotion to Yahweh was not secret, and there would be consequences. They were okay with that, even if they died for their convictions. They told the king, "If this be so, our God whom we serve is able to deliver us from the burning fiery furnace, and he will deliver us out of your hand, O king. But if not, be it known to you, O king, that we will not serve your gods or worship the golden image that you have set up" (Dan 3:17-18).

Daniel and his three friends were delivered from their threatening circumstances. But they did not speak to God presumptuously, as if they knew what the outcome would be. The three Hebrews rightly embodied the fear of the Lord. No matter what King Nebuchadnezzar threatened to do, they would be steadfast. If honoring the Lord meant dishonoring Nebuchadnezzar, then so be it. If honoring the Lord meant losing their lives, then so be it. All those who are wise will eventually die. Better, then, to trust the Lord and do what is wise. After all, God will raise the wise to life and glory.

THE WISE WHO SHINE

Part of the future hope of God's people is resurrection from the dead, and the book of Daniel talks about it.[2] In fact, Daniel 12:2 provides the clearest and boldest Old Testament promise of a general resurrection: "And many of those who sleep in the dust of the earth shall awake, some to everlasting life, and some to shame and everlasting contempt." Both the righteous and the wicked are in view. The future of the righteous is everlasting life, but the future of the wicked is everlasting judgment.

Before the promise in Daniel 12:2, a heavenly figure tells of a difficult future for God's people. They will face persecution under a vile and blasphemous ruler. This ruler

> shall seduce with flattery those who violate the covenant, but the people who know their God shall stand firm and take action. And the wise among the people shall make many understand, though for some days they shall stumble by sword and flame, by captivity and plunder. When they stumble, they shall receive a little help. And many shall join themselves to them with flattery, and some of the wise shall stumble, so that they may be refined, purified, and made white, until the time of the end, for it still awaits the appointed time. (Dan 11:32-35)

---

[2]For an exploration of resurrection hope in Scripture, see Mitchell L. Chase, *Resurrection Hope and the Death of Death*, Short Studies in Biblical Theology (Wheaton, IL: Crossway, 2022); M. Jeff Brannon, *The Hope of Life After Death: A Biblical Theology*, Essential Studies in Biblical Theology (Downers Grove, IL: IVP Academic, 2022).

Some of the teaching in Daniel 11:32-35 can be challenging to interpret, but certain features stand out. Those Israelites "who know their God" are the wise, and the Israelites "who violate the covenant" are the unrighteous. The covenant violators are seduced by flattery, by the voice of Lady Folly speaking through the vile ruler. The wise will not have it easy. They will face suffering, even death. Yet the Lord is refining and purifying them. They will be "made white"—cleansed and vindicated. According to Daniel 12:2, they will be *raised*.

We know the resurrection of the wise is in view because of the explicit language in the very next verse: "And those who are wise shall shine like the brightness of the sky above; and those who turn many to righteousness, like the stars forever and ever" (Dan 12:3). The resurrection of the dead will mean the glorification of the righteous. The wise will shine because of the power of God raising and glorifying their bodies.

The future of the wise is brightness and glory. The language of shining is more than a metaphor, though it is not less than that. Light is in contrast to darkness, and darkness is the abode of the wicked, those who do not know God. According to Daniel 11–12, those who forsake the covenant will reap forsakenness—a resurrection to shame and everlasting contempt (Dan 12:2), a resurrection to *judgment*. The brightness of the righteous is about their future reflection of divine glory, which they will reflect forever in their resurrected state.

A heart of wisdom belongs to a life in the light, so the bright future of the wise is fitting for such a person when the body is raised to rival the glory of the heavenly stars.

A WONDERFUL COUNSELOR

The need for the wayward nation is to be like Daniel and his three friends. The Israelites need to know that though the discipline of the Lord is coming, the exile will be temporary. They need to keep God's commandments and resist the seductive lies of Lady Folly and the foreign adversaries. Her lies are heard through the false prophets, who tell the people, "Sword and famine shall not come upon this land" (Jer 14:15). These false prophets are directly contradicting the Word of God. They speak like the serpent in Eden: "You will not surely die" (Gen 3:4).

But God appoints true prophets who tell hard truths about a coming judgment and a wrecked city and an exiled people. This will not be the last word, however. God's promise through his prophets is also about a future for his people, which transcends their current rebellion and spiritual decline. He says, for instance,

> I will heal their apostasy;
> I will love them freely,
> for my anger has turned from them.
> I will be like the dew to Israel;
> he shall blossom like the lily;
> he shall take root like the trees of Lebanon;
> his shoots shall spread out;
> his beauty shall be like the olive,
> and his fragrance like Lebanon.
> They shall return and dwell beneath my shadow;
> they shall flourish like the grain;
> they shall blossom like the vine;
> their fame shall be like the wine of Lebanon. (Hos 14:4-7)

In light of such a future, the Israelites should love God's commands and recoil against what the law forbids. Hosea says, "Whoever is wise, let him understand these things; whoever is discerning, let him know them; for the ways of the LORD are right, and the upright walk in them, but transgressors stumble in them" (Hos 14:9). This final verse of Hosea's prophecy is a call to wise living. Those with discernment will see the goodness and wisdom of God's commands and will walk accordingly. On the other hand, transgressors are fools, for they reject God's ways and do not walk according to his commands.

As Yahweh's corporate son, Israel needs to receive the divine rebuke and chastisement, for the sake of their future life and flourishing. And in the fullness of God's revelation, the promise of such flourishing will be the outworking of a new covenant. God will place his law within them, writing it on their very hearts, and in this new covenant, every member will know him and will experience the everlasting pardon of their sins (Jer 31:31-34).

The prophets associate this new covenant dynamic with the future Davidic king, whom God promised to David (see 2 Sam 7:12-13). This king, this Son of David, will lead God's new covenant people into their future of resurrection life and glory. He will bring light to those in darkness (Is 9:2). He will reign forever on David's throne (Is 9:6-7). And according to the prophets, this king will be wise.

The "shoot from the stump of Jesse" (Is 11:1), which is a phrase about the promised Davidic descendant, will have the Spirit of the Lord: "And the Spirit of the LORD shall rest upon him, the Spirit of wisdom and understanding, the Spirit of counsel and might, the Spirit of knowledge and the fear of the LORD" (Is 11:2).

This accumulation of phrases in Isaiah 11:2 is a description of a supremely wise person. The coming king will fulfill the expectations for the kind of king that the Torah holds out hope for (see Deut 17:14-20). He will be a greater ruler than Joseph or Daniel. He will be called "Wonderful Counselor, Mighty God, Everlasting Father, Prince of Peace" (Is 9:6). That first title is especially interesting for our purposes, because it is a wisdom title. A counselor provides counsel, direction, insight. Someone who is committed to the truth and who speaks the truth compellingly will be a Wonderful Counselor indeed.

Isaiah 9 is a prophecy about the birth of the Messiah, and this Davidic king will be characterized by wonderful counsel. His trustworthy insight will be guaranteed by the presence of the Holy Spirit on him (as promised in Is 11:2). Never has there been a king like this over Israel. And once this king arrives, no other king will ever be needed.

CONCLUSION

The author of 1–2 Kings narrates the spiritual decline of Yahweh's corporate son. A divided kingdom led to the rise of adversaries who would defeat God's people and carry them into exile. This divine judgment was just, for the people had worshiped idols and committed abominations, rejecting God's wisdom and righteous ways. Instead of walking uprightly, the people chose a crooked path.

A fractured and declining kingdom did not mean all hope was lost, however. People like Daniel dwelled in Babylon, and their devotion to Yahweh was like a holy fire burning in the suffocating darkness of captivity. Despite threats from kings and others in powerful positions, the wise feared the Lord and endured their opponents. The wise could count on God's vindication, certainly at the future judgment and resurrection, but even in the present life if God was pleased to confound worldly wisdom and to overturn political might. The path of rebellion led to judgment, because the words of Lady Folly did not have the best interests of the people at heart. A rejection of the covenant reaped the curses of the covenant. The Israelites were riddled with ungodly worship and unrighteous kings. They needed a new covenant and a new king. This new covenant would deliver them from their deepest exile, and this new king would have the voice of a shepherd to lead the wise into their bright future of shining glory.

Chapter Ten

SOMETHING GREATER THAN SOLOMON

WHAT WORDS WOULD YOU USE to describe Jesus? If we study the stories in the Gospels, we see that Jesus is compassionate, for he ministers to the outcasts and has pity on those in need. He is bold, for he confronts religious leaders and scribes even though they are highly esteemed in the eyes of the Jews. He is patient, for he welcomes individuals and circumstances that seem inconvenient to his disciples.

Those are all warranted descriptions of Jesus, and the list could go on. Have you thought much about Jesus' wisdom? The Gospel stories demonstrate that, throughout his earthly ministry, Jesus was *wise*—supremely wise in his words and in his deeds.

In a study such as this one that explores what the biblical authors teach about wisdom, we must talk about Jesus. We must hear and read the words of David's greatest Son.

FIRST VERSE AND FIRST CHAPTER

When we turn the page from Malachi 4 to Matthew 1, four hundred years of history elapse between the events in those chapters. The Old Testament era came to a close with Malachi as the final prophet before those four centuries of prophetic silence commenced. After Malachi's ministry, the kingdom of God has not come, the Messiah has not been born, and the nation of Israel is still in spiritual strife. But four hundred years after Malachi, the silence is broken.

The Gospel of Matthew is ready to tell the story of the one known as Jesus of Nazareth. The first chapter of the first New Testament book gives the genealogical background for Jesus. He is indeed a descendant of David. The Davidic emphasis is clear from the very first verse of the New Testament: "The book of the genealogy of Jesus Christ, the son of David, the son of Abraham" (Mt 1:1). Jesus' Davidic pedigree is the subject of the genealogy in Matthew 1:2-16.

Calling Jesus the "son of David" (Mt 1:1) is not only something this Gospel writer does. Matthew reports this language on the lips of others. At the triumphal entry in Matthew 21, people from the crowds shout, "Hosanna to the Son of David! Blessed is he who comes in the name of the Lord! Hosanna in the highest!" (Mt 21:9). Before Jesus gives sight to Bartimaeus, the blind beggar calls out, "Jesus, Son of David, have mercy on me!" (Mk 10:47). The title "son of David" is important for the Gospels because it directly ties Jesus to the promise in 2 Samuel 7:12-13, of David's offspring one day being born to rule on the throne forever.

Besides being a title, the "son of David" language reminds us of Solomon, for Solomon was a son of David. In 1 Kings 1–11, we read of Solomon's reign and wisdom. By calling Jesus the "son of David," the Gospels are helping us remember both the hope for the Messiah and that David's immediate son Solomon *was not* this Messiah. Other descendants—sons—of David reigned in Jerusalem after Solomon, but they were not *the* Son of David. Being on the lookout for David's greater and greatest son, interpreters hear the joyful sound of Matthew's declaration that Jesus is the Christ, the long-awaited Davidic king. At last, something greater than Solomon is here.

THE OBEDIENT SON

As we read the stories about Jesus in the Gospels, we get the distinct impression that he was an obedient son. This truth is also borne out by the letters of the

New Testament, such as Hebrews 4:15, which says he "has been tempted as we are, yet without sin," or Hebrews 5:8, which says, "Although he was a son, he learned obedience through what he suffered."

In the case of Hebrews 5:8, the learning of obedience was not something that happened after disobedience. The faithfulness and sinlessness of Jesus comprised his obedient life, and this "learning" was something that pertained to his genuine humanity. He truly faced temptation, he truly suffered, and he truly overcame these things with utter sinlessness in his heart, words, and actions.

Jesus was the obedient Son. Having an obedient son is a key theme in Proverbs, as we have seen. Solomon says, "A wise son makes a glad father, but a foolish son is a sorrow to his mother" (Prov 10:1). Jesus was always a wise, and never foolish, son. He was the paragon of someone growing in wisdom and discernment.

Luke's Gospel gives us insight into the young life of Jesus, but not because Luke tells us many stories. Regarding specific events, we read an infancy narrative (Lk 1:26-38; 2:1-20), a statement that Jesus was circumcised (Lk 2:21), the presentation of baby Jesus at the temple (Lk 2:22-38), and a situation in Jerusalem when Jesus was twelve years old (Lk 2:41-52). While each of these parts in Luke 1–2 is worth prolonged contemplation, the narrator's summary statements are perhaps just as profound. According to Luke 2:40, "the child grew and became strong, filled with wisdom. And the favor of God was upon him" (Lk 2:40).

The description in Luke 2:40 fits with the theme of an obedient son. In Proverbs, God blesses the obedient son, and the wise walk in God's favor. We learn that Jesus, being truly human, grew and became strong, but this growth was not just physical. Jesus was "filled with wisdom." This phrase corresponds to the Old Testament promise about the coming Messiah, that the Spirit of wisdom and understanding would be on him (Is 11:2).

Jesus' growth in wisdom was the result of parental instruction, for Mary and Joseph were faithful examples of Torah obedience (Mt 1:19; Lk 1:38; 2:22, 39, 41). The father in Proverbs says, "Hear, my son, your father's instruction, and forsake not your mother's teaching" (Prov 1:8), and such a son would be embodied by the Lord Jesus, who never forsook the instruction he received. According to his humanity, Jesus learned, internalized, and obeyed.

The story of young Jesus at the temple (when he was twelve) ends with the narrator telling us, "And he went down with them and came to Nazareth and was submissive to them. And his mother treasured up all these things in her heart" (Lk 2:51). His submission to Joseph and Mary was a keeping of the fifth commandment, that children should honor their father and mother (Ex 20:12). Jesus' actions toward them were honorable and never sinful. His total obedience was important because he came not to abolish the Law or the Prophets but to fulfill them (Mt 5:17). Part of keeping the commands of God involved his submission to the adult authorities in the home.

Luke tells us again of Jesus' growth. In Nazareth, "Jesus increased in wisdom and in stature and in favor with God and man" (Lk 2:52). This is a fuller description than what we read in Luke 2:40, where "the child grew and became strong, filled with wisdom. And the favor of God was upon him." According to Luke 2:52, the truly human Jesus was wise before God and humankind. He experienced the blessing and favor of walking rightly with others. As the obedient Son, he was a blessing to his earthly parents, and he was the delight of his heavenly Father (Mk 1:11).

CHRIST THE SAGE

Using the book of Proverbs as a template, we see not only the theme of the obedient son but also the theme of the wise instructor. The father in Proverbs gives insight for living in the fear of the Lord. His instruction is not merely experiential. The teachings are based on what God has revealed in earlier Scripture and in general revelation.

Because the father in Proverbs is wise, he is a sage for his son and for all who read his work. This instructor role is something Jesus himself embodies. He is a teacher. He is certainly more than a teacher, but he is not less than that.[1] At the beginning of his earthly ministry, he travels and gathers crowds and preaches.

---

[1] For a book-length treatment of this topic, see Jonathan T. Pennington, *Jesus the Great Philosopher: Rediscovering the Wisdom Needed for the Good Life* (Grand Rapids, MI: Brazos, 2020).

How early were Jesus' wise words evident? The four Gospels do not give us a particular age, but you will recall that in Luke 2:40, 52, Jesus grew and increased in wisdom and favor with God and humankind. When he was twelve years old in the temple, he was "sitting among the teachers, listening to them and asking them questions. And all who heard him were amazed at his understanding and his answers" (Lk 2:46-47).

Though we do not know all the details of that temple scene in Luke 2:46-49, we can conclude a few things. First, Jesus' questions were not from his ignorance. He was probably asking questions to the teachers in order to provoke their thinking and reflection. Second, Jesus demonstrated understanding to these teachers, and they were amazed. We know, then, that Jesus' words revealed his knowledge, and apparently his knowledge was profound. Third, the teachers were amazed at Jesus' "answers," which suggests some kind of instruction that he provided. Maybe these answers were in response to questions from the teachers, or perhaps Jesus was posing questions and then answering them. Either way, he was not like any other twelve-year-old they had known. Fourth, Jesus' discernment had already exceeded that of his parents. When Mary and Joseph found him in the temple, he said to them, "Why were you looking for me? Did you not know that I must be in my Father's house?" (Lk 2:49). According to Luke, they did not understand the saying that Jesus had spoken to them (Lk 2:50). This was a sign of things to come, which would unfold on a deeper level and on a much larger scale.

As the Gospels report Jesus' teachings, they include some staggering claims from his lips, and one of these claims invokes David's son. In Matthew 12 Jesus is teaching about the future resurrection and judgment, and he says, "The queen of the South will rise up at the judgment with this generation and condemn it, for she came from the ends of the earth to hear the wisdom of Solomon, and behold, something greater than Solomon is here" (Mt 12:42). Given what we know of Solomon's vast wisdom (1 Kings 3:11-12), Jesus' claim about himself should give us pause. If Solomon was great not only because he was a king but because he was supremely wise, then Jesus' claim is an assertion of his supremacy over Solomon. Jesus is claiming to be wiser than the wisest man who ever lived. Now that is either one of the most foolish things someone could utter, or it is not foolish because it is true.

In 1 Kings 10, the queen (to whom Jesus refers in Mt 12:42) was from Sheba, and she traveled to see Solomon because she heard of his great fame and wisdom (1 Kings 10:1, 6-7). She arrived with hard questions (1 Kings 10:1) and gifts (1 Kings 10:2). She brought "a very great retinue, with camels bearing spices and very much gold and precious stones" (1 Kings 10:2). She gave Solomon "120 talents of gold, and a very great quantity of spices and precious stones. Never again came such an abundance of spices as these that the queen of Sheba gave to King Solomon" (1 Kings 10:10).

The queen's journey and gifts to Solomon are echoed in the early life of Jesus, the one greater than Solomon. The queen was a Gentile from a different land, and she came with gifts to the king, gifts that included gold and spices. Does this make you think of the magi who come to visit Jesus in Matthew 2? According to Matthew 2:1, "wise men from the east came to Jerusalem," looking for the king of the Jews. When they arrive at the right home in Bethlehem, "they saw the child with Mary his mother, and they fell down and worshiped him. Then, opening their treasures, they offered him gifts, gold and frankincense and myrrh" (Mt 2:11). With ears tuned to hear Old Testament echoes, we notice that, like the queen of Sheba, these magi are Gentiles from another land, and they come to offer gifts to the son of David. But these wise men bow before the Wiser One, the greater Solomon.

The wisdom of Jesus is evident during his teaching ministry. People call him things such as "Good Teacher" (Mk 10:17) or "Rabbi" (Mt 26:25), even though Jesus never attended rabbinical school. These titles nevertheless demonstrate the impression Jesus gives to people. He is a teacher, a *sage*. The chief subject of his instruction is the kingdom of God (Mt 4:17; Mk 1:14-15). This subject dominates his parables as well. He teaches parables in order to show who is "in" and who is "out," in terms of spiritual understanding and kingdom membership (Mk 4:11-12).

The four Gospels report lengthy teaching discourses from Jesus the Sage. Perhaps the most famous one is the Sermon on the Mount, found in Matthew 5–7. But other places—such as Matthew 13; Mark 4; Luke 6; and John 6—have long discourse sections as well. These discourses consist of different topics, images, and rhetorical devices. Jesus is a master teacher. Some synagogue attendees once say, "A new teaching with authority!"

(Mk 1:27). Some religious officers once say, "No one ever spoke like this man!" (Jn 7:46). According to Matthew 7:28-29, "the crowds were astonished at his teaching, for he was teaching them as one who had authority, and not as their scribes."

The sage role of Jesus is especially evident near the end of Matthew 7, as he teaches with binary ideas. He speaks of a narrow way and a broad way, one that leads to life and the other that leads to destruction (Mt 7:13-14), and he speaks about wise and foolish builders (Mt 7:24-27). These categories are rooted in the wisdom texts of the Old Testament, such as Proverbs, where Solomon teaches about two ways that lead to different ends. Therefore, Jesus calls people to wisdom and away from folly. He is the wise teacher whose words must be heard and heeded. But his teachings also need to be spiritually discerned. He says things such as, "He who has ears, let him hear" (Mt 13:9).

Fools show their foolishness by resisting Jesus' teachings and by continuing in disobedience. During Passion Week in Jerusalem, some people come to Jesus with questions to trap him in his words (Mt 21–22). But Jesus avoids their traps. He answers with discernment and wisdom. For example, when asked about paying taxes to Caesar, he responds in such a way that when the questioners hear his answer, "they marveled. And they left him and went away" (Mt 22:22). Such a response shows his superior understanding as he evades the poisonous snares of the deceitful and hypocritical speakers. Jesus' wisdom is so great that he can discern the hearts of those he encounters (Mk 2:8; Jn 2:24-25).

WISDOM IN THE FLESH

So far in this chapter, we have considered that Jesus is the obedient and wise Son and thus the recipient and pursuer of wisdom. He is also the sage or teacher, and thus he is the dispenser of wisdom. He internalizes and instructs. He embodies the wise life as someone who loves wisdom, practices wisdom, and teaches wisdom. His heart is rightly ordered. When we look at the ethical duties in the book of Proverbs, we are looking into the perfect heart of Christ.

Because of Christ's heart and life of wisdom, we can see why Paul would say that in Christ "are hidden all the treasures of wisdom and knowledge" (Col 2:3). He says that Christ "became to us wisdom from God, righteousness and sanctification and redemption" (1 Cor 1:30). So Christ not only pursues wisdom and teaches wisdom; he *is* wisdom—Wisdom from God.

Have you considered the similarity between Christ's teachings and the voice of Wisdom in Proverbs? The personification of wisdom in Proverbs is Lady Wisdom, and the feminine depiction is due to the feminine gender of the noun for wisdom. That grammatical fact does not prevent us from noticing that the pleas of Lady Wisdom are echoed in the words of Jesus of Nazareth.

Jesus says that people should come to him so that they will have life. Do you see what a distinct teaching this is, compared with other philosophers in the ancient world who pointed people to a wise path? Jesus wants people to lay down their nets and follow him, not just so that they will *learn* from him but so that they will *have life* in him (Mt 4:19; Jn 8:12).

When Wisdom calls to those in the marketplaces, the voice says, "If you turn at my reproof, behold, I will pour out my spirit to you; I will make my words known to you" (Prov 1:23). Those who listen to Wisdom's voice will dwell secure (Prov 1:33). Wisdom has life and peace for those who listen and obey (Prov 3:16-18). Wisdom says, "Come, eat of my bread and drink of the wine I have mixed. Leave your simple ways, and live, and walk in the way of insight" (Prov 9:5-6).

The voice of Jesus is not just the personification of Wisdom; it is the incarnation of Wisdom. Jesus calls people to hear his words and follow his way. He promises to pour out his Spirit on his disciples. He holds out bread and wine and declares that they represent his body and blood, which he will lay down for sinners. As the Wisdom of God, the Lord Jesus has come to save sinners from the darkness of folly and the outcome of destruction.

When Jesus says, "Repent, for the kingdom of heaven is at hand" (Mt 4:17), he is calling people to turn from folly and to pursue the life of the kingdom—a life found *in him*. Jesus says, "I am the light of the world. Whoever follows me will not walk in darkness, but will have the light of life" (Jn 8:12). He is the Good Shepherd, whose voice calls to his sheep as he leads them into everlasting life: "I am the good shepherd. I know my own and my own know me, just as the Father knows me and I know the Father; and I lay down my life for the sheep. And I have other sheep that are not of this fold. I must bring them also, and they will listen to my voice. So there will be one flock, one shepherd" (Jn 10:14-16). Jesus is the voice of Wisdom guiding his sheep into green pastures and still waters (Ps 23:2).

The personification of Wisdom in Proverbs 8 is especially interesting in light of the incarnation. In Proverbs 8:22-23, Wisdom was present at creation, before the beginning of all things. Wisdom was "brought forth" (Prov 8:24), as if begotten by God. According to Proverbs 8, Wisdom was before all things, and without Wisdom nothing was made that has been made. This reasoning is like John 1: "In the beginning was the Word, and the Word was with God, and the Word was God. He was in the beginning with God. All things were made through him, and without him was not any thing made that was made" (Jn 1:1-3). Everything John wrote about the Word we can say about Wisdom.

And in the fullness of time, the Wisdom of God became flesh and dwelled among us.

WAY, TRUTH, AND LIFE

Jesus is the obedient Son, he is the wise sage, and he is divine Wisdom. He understands himself to be the source of wisdom and thus the source of life. If people want life, they must follow Christ. He tells his disciples, "I am the way, and the truth, and the life. No one comes to the Father except through me" (Jn 14:6).

This "I am" claim reverberates with wisdom echoes. Wisdom passages in the Old Testament (such as in Proverbs) are concerned about the "way" a person goes. There is the way of wisdom and the way of folly, and these two paths end in different places. Jesus' claim is that he is the way. The way of folly is the way of falsehood, which means the path of wisdom is the path of truth. Jesus is the one we should follow, and he is the truth we should confess. He is the way and the truth. Where does the path of wisdom lead? To life and blessing. If Jesus is the way and truth, he must also be the life, for there can be no wise way and divine truth that does not lead to life. Jesus is all three. He is the life to receive, the truth to believe, and the way to walk.

The language in John 14:6 is the kind of claim we would expect from the voice of Wisdom in Proverbs. Knowing what we do about the personification of Wisdom in that book, we would not be surprised if Wisdom said, "I am the way and the truth and the life." How significant, then, that this claim is on the lips of Jesus, who is the embodiment of Wisdom, the source of life and blessing. He is the trustworthy teacher. He not only knows the path to life; he *is* the path.

Jesus' disciples may not have understood everything Jesus taught during his earthly ministry, but they were beginning to grasp some major truths about who he was and what he came to give. Once while he has been teaching hard things to the crowds, some people turn away and no longer walk with him (Jn 6:60-66). So Jesus asks his twelve disciples, "Do you want to go away as well?" (Jn 6:67). After all, when Wisdom is speaking in the streets and calling for the passersby to hear and to heed, some people may think the voice of Wisdom speaks too many hard things and that following the path of Wisdom is too difficult.

Peter answers Jesus' question, "Lord, to whom shall we go? You have the words of eternal life, and we have believed, and have come to know, that you are the Holy One of God" (Jn 6:68-69). The words of Jesus are the words of Wisdom, because the words of Wisdom are the words of life—*eternal* life. The more we understand about who Jesus is, the more we will see the pinpoint accuracy of Peter's answer.

WHAT THE WISE DO

What we do with Jesus will show whether we are wise or foolish. More specifically, what we do with his words, those words of eternal life, will show what kind of builder we are. His voice is the voice of Wisdom, and we need to respond rightly to him.

Near the end of the Sermon on the Mount, Jesus says,

> Everyone then who hears these words of mine and does them will be like a wise man who built his house on the rock. And the rain fell, and the floods came, and the winds blew and beat on that house, but it did not fall, because it had been founded on the rock. And everyone who hears these words of mine and does not do them will be like a foolish man who built his house on the sand. And the rain fell, and the floods came, and the winds blew and beat against that house, and it fell, and great was the fall of it. (Mt 7:24-27)

This instruction is one of Jesus' most famous teachings. He is addressing people who will face the judgment of God. The context of final judgment is established by the previous language of destruction versus life (Mt 7:13-14), the diseased tree being cut down and thrown into the fire (Mt 7:19), and workers of lawlessness departing from Christ (Mt 7:21-23). In Matthew 7:24-27, the arrival of the rain and floods and winds is the arrival of divine judgment. The righteous will stand in the judgment because they are those who have responded in faith to Christ. The wicked, however, will not stand in the judgment, because they have rejected Christ and his words.

Jesus teaches that what happens at the final judgment will depend on what you do with his words here and now. If you hear him and then reject what he said, you are a fool. If you hear him and then live in light of what he said, you are wise. According to Jesus, then, wisdom is not just hearing his words; it is heeding them, building according to them. Fools are those who listen to what Jesus says and then do whatever they want. They do what is right in their own eyes instead of responding to the words of Christ with faith and delight.

The scene pictured in Matthew 7:24-27 is thematically similar to Psalm 1, where the Blessed Man rejects false words and delights in God's words (Ps 1:1-2). Because he is wise and knows the Lord, the Blessed Man will stand with the congregation of the righteous, while the wicked are like chaff that is driven away by the wind (Ps 1:4-6). The path of the wicked leads to destruction (Ps 1:6), but those who build their lives on the words of Christ will stand vindicated on the rock when the judgment comes.

When we read Psalm 1 in light of Matthew 7:24-27, our delight in God's words will include the teachings of Christ and about Christ. Jesus is the way, the truth, and the life (Jn 14:6). There is no way to the Father but through him, and there is no foundation that stands secure through the righteous judgment of God but the solid rock of his words.

CONCLUSION

In the four Gospels, Jesus is the promised Davidic king and the one greater than Solomon. Solomon was incredibly wise, but Jesus' greatness is about a wisdom even more supreme than Solomon's. Jesus is the all-wise king who is full of the Spirit and who is the consummate sage. His words are always true and are therefore always trustworthy. Besides being the perfect teacher, he is the obedient Son who has internalized God's words and delights in all that is good and true and wise. Indeed, Christ *is* the Wisdom of God. His voice summons disciples and leads his sheep.

If people turn to the incarnate Wisdom of God, they will know the life and blessing that comes from his hand. Jesus is the very source of eternal life. When we read his teachings and hear his claims, we get the distinct impression that Jesus' words are a firm foundation for sinners to find life and refuge. Those who trust Jesus will not perish but will have everlasting life. They will have this kind of life because they have Jesus, and they have Jesus because they responded to his words and built their lives on the solid rock.

All other ground is sinking sand.

Chapter Eleven

WALKING WISELY IN EVIL DAYS

IN A FALLEN WORLD, a life of wisdom is countercultural. How could it not be? We continue to deal with indwelling sins, external snares of temptation, opponents to the Christian faith, demonic deceptions, and satanic predation. Paul surveys life under the sun and says, "The days are evil" (Eph 5:16). This truth about these days is not the only thing we can say about them. God is mightily at work, the gospel is powerful to save, the kingdom of Christ has been inaugurated under the sun, and the church of Christ will overcome the evil one by the blood of the Lamb.

Though these are evil days, we have the strengthening and sustaining Spirit of the Lord at work in us and through us. Getting the fuller picture from Paul's earlier claim, he says, "Look carefully then how you walk, not as unwise but as wise, making the best use of the time, because the days are evil" (Eph 5:15-16).

It is possible that people will walk—or live—unwisely in evil days. That must not be the case for Christians. We must walk wisely, paying attention to our path.

RENEWED IMAGE BEARERS

In our old life in Adam, we failed to be faithful image bearers. Though made in the image of God, we followed our deceitful desires and did not love the Lord with all our heart, soul, mind, and strength. Our old life did not bear the fruit of the Spirit. Our old life was not lived for the glory of God. Our old life was not on the path of wisdom.

But according to Paul, we are being "renewed in the spirit of your minds" (Eph 4:23). The work of the Holy Spirit is in our spirits. This renewal is enabling us to think and see differently. Such transformation leads to discernment: "that by testing you may discern what is the will of God, what is good and acceptable and perfect" (Rom 12:2). The inner work of the Spirit helps us see the truth and goodness of what God has revealed.

The Spirit's renewing work is grounded in our new standing with God, and our new standing with God is the result of our new self, the new person. This new person is "created after the likeness of God in true righteousness and holiness" (Eph 4:24). In the phrase "created after the likeness of God," we hear the echo of Genesis 1:26. God said, "Let us make man in our image, after our likeness" (Gen 1:26). So God created male and female in his image (Gen 1:27). According to Genesis 5:1, "When God created man, he made him in the likeness of God."

God blessed and commissioned his image bearers to be fruitful and to have dominion (Gen 1:28). With the entrance of sin and death into the world, God's image bearers have been unable to fulfill all that God had made them for and commissioned them to do. Their fruitfulness and dominion are not uncorrupted under the sun. Rather, because of sin's effects on the human heart, the history of humankind is a long story of idolatry and the wages of sin.

In the first Adam, we fell short of the glory of God. But in the last Adam, we have been redeemed, we are being renewed, and we will be glorified. The "new self" is "created after the likeness of God" (Eph 4:24). Desmond Alexander says, "By becoming a perfect human viceregent in the present, Jesus Christ is able to re-establish the viceregent status of other human beings in the future. In doing so, Christ may be considered a 'second Adam.'"[1] We are

---

[1] T. Desmond Alexander, *From Eden to the New Jerusalem: An Introduction to Biblical Theology* (Grand Rapids, MI: Kregel Academic, 2008), 94.

learning to be image bearers again, in the fullest and deepest sense. We have become true worshipers of the living God. We are becoming, in Christ, new Adams and Eves who will reign with Christ. Sanctification is preparing us for full dominion, to rule as kings and queens in a new creation.

Though sin affected our ability to live out our image-bearing status, this task is recovered and renewed in Christ. Our new self "is being renewed in knowledge after the image of its creator" (Col 3:10). We have come to truly know the living God, and because of our union with Christ, we will grow in wisdom as transformed image bearers. We must no longer rebel against the Lord's authority as the first Adam did. We must welcome God's commands and submit to his will. Being a renewed image bearer means living out a love for God in all of life.

GROWING IN WISDOM IN CHRIST

The New Testament letters are filled with indicatives and directives for the Christian life. Sometimes an author organizes a writing to have that kind of structural flow, such as Romans 1–11 and Romans 12–16, or even Ephesians 1–3 and Ephesians 4–6. We need to understand what God has done and why and how, and we need to understand how to respond and live in light of what he has done.

Walking wisely is the fruit of saving faith. It is working out our salvation with fear and trembling (Phil 2:12). The reason we know such fruit will come is that we are united to Christ. Union with Christ is salvation, and vice versa. Because of our new covenant life in the Son of God, we will bear fruit that corresponds to such new life.

A metaphor Jesus gives for our fruit bearing is the vine and its branches. Jesus is the true vine (Jn 15:1), and the disciples are the branches (Jn 15:5). He says, "I am the vine; you are the branches. Whoever abides in me and I in him, he it is that bears much fruit, for apart from me you can do nothing" (Jn 15:5). The key is our life in Christ, and it is an eternal status that has already begun. Believers are already "in Christ" (Rom 8:1). We have been crucified with him and now we live in him (Gal 2:20).

Our life in Christ will mean growth in wisdom because of the Spirit's ongoing work within us. In fact, one way to describe the wise disciple's life is with the fruit of the Spirit. Paul says, "The fruit of the Spirit is love, joy, peace, patience, kindness, goodness, faithfulness, gentleness, self-control" (Gal 5:22-23). A wise heart wants to be rightly ordered and to walk in step with the gospel. The fruit of the Spirit is appealing to the wise person because the wise know the beauty of a life being lived for God's glory and our good.

Though wisdom beautifies, folly corrupts and contorts. A life of folly is shaped like the acts of the flesh. Paul says that "the works of the flesh are evident: sexual immorality, impurity, sensuality, idolatry, sorcery, enmity, strife, jealousy, fits of anger, rivalries, dissensions, divisions, envy, drunkenness, orgies, and things like these. I warn you, as I warned you before, that those who do such things will not inherit the kingdom of God" (Gal 5:19-21).

When we believe the lies of Lady Folly, the works of the flesh are the result. But when we trust Christ and build our lives on the solid rock of his words, the fruit of the Spirit produces a life of vitality and spiritual strength. Paul tells the Philippians, "And it is my prayer that your love may abound more and more, with knowledge and all discernment, so that you may approve what is excellent, and so be pure and blameless for the day of Christ, filled with the fruit of righteousness that comes through Jesus Christ, to the glory and praise of God" (Phil 1:9-11).

We need to be able to discern and approve "what is excellent," and that will only happen through our growth in godliness and wisdom. This is Paul's prayer for the Philippians. He asks God for their love and wisdom to abound. He can pray with confidence about such a thing because of what the Lord has already begun in them. The Lord will complete what he started (Phil 1:6), and the process of Christian growth will involve growth in wisdom.

Christians are new people (2 Cor 5:17). They have "put off the old self" and "have put on the new self" (Col 3:9-10). The old self was who they were in Adam, and the new self is who they are in Christ. The new self is Christ. We put on the new self (positionally) at salvation. We have died, been buried, and raised with Christ (Rom 6:2-4). We also put on the new self (progressively) through sanctification. Paul tells the Ephesians they were taught "to put off your old self, which belongs to your former manner of life and is corrupt through deceitful desires, and to be renewed in the spirit of your minds, and to put on the new self, created after the likeness of God in true righteousness and holiness" (Eph 4:22-24).

CHRIST FOR ALL OF LIFE

The disciple's life is under the lordship of Christ, as all things are. Yet for the disciple, Christ's lordship is not a thing to be resisted or a reality to be bemoaned. Christ's lordship is good news for sinners, and it is the banner under which we walk the path of life.

Like the writer of Proverbs, the apostle Paul desires that believers grow in wisdom and righteousness and the fear of the Lord. Paul tells the Corinthians, "Let us cleanse ourselves from every defilement of body and spirit, bringing holiness to completion in the fear of God" (2 Cor 7:1). This cleansing is an act of dominion, an exercise over body and spirit, for the sake of holiness. Cleansing our lives of sinful practices is something a renewed image bearer wants and does.

Living wisely is like training. It takes deliberation and discipline. It requires commitment and sacrifice. Paul tells Timothy, "Train yourself for godliness; for while bodily training is of some value, godliness is of value in every way, as it holds promise for the present life and also for the life to come" (1 Tim 4:7-8). Wisdom is not for this life only. The fear of the Lord matters because this life is not all there is.

When Paul tells the Ephesians, "Look carefully then how you walk, not as unwise but as wise" (Eph 5:15), such carefulness is warranted because of the deceitfulness of sin. The days are evil (Eph 5:16). "Therefore do not be foolish, but understand what the will of the Lord is" (Eph 5:17). God has called his people to a certain manner of living, and folly is not part of it. Folly inhibits the Christian life, and it affects those we are called to love.

Before addressing relationships in the household in Ephesians 5:22–6:9, Paul wants believers in the local church to "be filled with the Spirit, addressing one another in psalms and hymns and spiritual songs, singing and making melody to the Lord with your heart, giving thanks always and for everything to God the Father in the name of our Lord Jesus Christ, submitting to one another out of reverence for Christ" (Eph 5:18-21). The closing phrase ("reverence for Christ") is about the fear of the Lord. But significantly, the

Lord is identified as the Lord Jesus. Reverence for the Savior is a heart disposition from which the proper treatment of others will flow.

Putting off our old and irreverent life in Adam, we have put on the new self, and now we walk in reverence for Christ. In reverence for Christ, we care about holiness and we desire to turn from wickedness. This posture is to encompass all of life. We are no longer darkened in our understanding or alienated from God (Eph 4:18). Growing in wisdom, and out of reverence for Christ, we put away falsehood (Eph 4:25), we do not indulge unrighteous anger (Eph 4:26), we do not steal (Eph 4:28), and we do not speak corruptible things (Eph 4:29).

In reverence for Christ, we want to be imitators of God (Eph 5:1), image bearers being renewed in love and life. We want to walk as children of light (Eph 5:8), seeking to discern with wisdom what pleases the Lord (Eph 5:10). The wise want to honor God and keep his commandments. So when we are tempted by the unfruitful works of darkness, we are to take no part in them (Eph 5:11). We are to reject evil because we are the children of light. Walking in reverence for Christ is what life in the light looks like.

Obedience to the Lord has implications for the household. Children are to obey their parents (Eph 6:1), and Paul shows the rightness of this instruction by quoting the fifth commandment (Eph 6:2-3). Obedience to parents is an important theme in Proverbs as well. The new covenant life does not leave these moral instructions behind. Taking our cues from Old Testament exhortations, we are to instruct our children and point them to the Lord. "Fathers," Paul says, "do not provoke your children to anger, but bring them up in the discipline and instruction of the Lord" (Eph 6:4).

Pointing children to wisdom and directing them in the ways of the Lord, we are imitating the Lord, who fathers us with utter faithfulness and love. Suffering and hostility can lead to weariness and faintheartedness, but we are nevertheless children whom God loves. His love for us is parental in the best of ways because he works for both our present *and* our everlasting good. The Lord disciplines those he loves (Prov 3:12), so he disciplines the disciples of Christ. The writer of Hebrews says, "It is for discipline that you have to endure. God is treating you as sons. For what son is there whom his father does not discipline? If you are left without discipline, in which all have participated, then you are illegitimate children and not sons" (Heb 12:7-8).

The author of Hebrews quotes Proverbs 3:11-12 (in Heb 12:5-6) and applies its reasoning to the new covenant community. The earthly parent (who fears the Lord) wants a child to walk in wisdom, and faithful discipline and proof are crucial to direct the child away from folly. The writer says that earthly parents "disciplined us for a short time as it seemed best to them, but he disciplines us for our good, that we may share his holiness. For the moment all discipline seems painful rather than pleasant, but later it yields the peaceful fruit of righteousness to those who have been trained by it" (Heb 12:10-11). The "he" who "disciplines us for our good" is the Lord, and the goal of divine discipline is the sharing in divine holiness.

True wisdom is more than financial stewardship and hard work, though these things are certainly included. We know people who do not fear God and yet they are good with money and dedicated to their vocation. Biblical wisdom—what James calls "wisdom from above" (Jas 3:17)—is connected to character and the posture of the heart. "The wisdom from above is first pure, then peaceable, gentle, open to reason, full of mercy and good fruits, impartial and sincere. And a harvest of righteousness is sown in peace by those who make peace" (Jas 3:17-18).

Believers need wisdom because they need to know how to conduct themselves. Paul tells the Colossians, "Walk in wisdom toward outsiders, making the best use of the time. Let your speech always be gracious, seasoned with salt, so that you may know how you ought to answer each person" (Col 4:5-6). What do we need to be light and salt for those around us? We need wisdom. What do we need to be faithful witnesses toward those outside the Christian faith? We need wisdom.

Paul's exhortation to the Colossians (in Col 4:5-6) is like what he tells the Ephesians: "Look carefully then how you walk, not as unwise but as wise, making the best use of the time, because the days are evil" (Eph 5:15-16). The wisdom we need does not originate from the world. It is truly wisdom from above.

IF ANYONE LACKS WISDOM

We need wisdom beyond the sun for life under the sun, and that means we must depend on the Lord. The letter of James—a document drenched with wisdom—opens with the recognition of trials and sufferings for the disciples of Christ. James calls for his readers to count trials a joy because of what God is doing through them, not because trials in themselves are good. "Count it all joy, my brothers, when you meet trials of various kinds, for you know that the testing of your faith produces steadfastness. And let steadfastness have its full effect, that you may be perfect and complete, lacking in nothing" (Jas 1:2-4).

The path of growing in wisdom will involve enduring the sufferings and trials that are part of this life and that are unique to a life devoted to Christ Jesus. But navigating the trials of life is no easy feat. The maturation of the believer requires wisdom, and wisdom comes from God. So James says, "If any of you lacks wisdom, let him ask God, who gives generously to all without reproach, and it will be given him" (Jas 1:5).

The fear of the Lord is the beginning of wisdom, and prayer to the Lord is the cry for wisdom. Those who have reverence for Christ will come to the Father in the name of Christ, seeking understanding and help and grace. We do not always know what to do in a given situation, because not all choices are a clear moral right or wrong. We need wisdom for both moral *and* nonmoral matters. And we need prayerful dependence on the Lord, that the Spirit might produce holy character in our hearts and lives.

James asks and answers, "Who is wise and understanding among you? By his good conduct let him show his works in the meekness of wisdom" (Jas 3:13). The wisdom that is "earthly, unspiritual, demonic" is characterized by jealousy and selfish ambition (Jas 3:14-15). Such inner attitudes will result in "disorder and every vile practice" (Jas 3:16). What is needed, therefore, is the wisdom that is from above, from heaven. The heavenly source is another way of saying that it is the wisdom of Christ. This wisdom "from above is first pure, then peaceable, gentle, open to reason, full of mercy and good fruits, impartial and sincere. And a harvest of righteousness is sown in peace by those who make peace" (Jas 3:17-18).

Even in the Old Testament, the people of God are to be a prayerful and wisdom-seeking people. They are to call out for insight and raise their voice for understanding (Prov 2:3). Or, to use James's words, the people of God are to call on their God. They should seek wisdom, for "the LORD gives wisdom;

from his mouth come knowledge and understanding" (Prov 2:6). They should seek, for the Lord gives. They should call out, for the Lord answers. He knows we need wisdom for evil days. We have a great high priest who dwells in heaven, and he sympathizes with us in our weaknesses (Heb 4:14-15). We can draw near to the throne of grace to receive help, as well as wisdom, in our time of need.

The fool does not depend on the Lord. The fool rests content on his own understanding. The fool does what is right in his own eyes, so prayer to the Lord is out of the question. The fool's conceit is an obstacle to the humble posture of fervent prayer. The fool thinks highly of himself and little of the consequences of sin or the snares of temptation. Therefore Paul says, "Let anyone who thinks that he stands take heed lest he fall. No temptation has overtaken you that is not common to man. God is faithful, and he will not let you be tempted beyond your ability, but with the temptation he will also provide the way of escape, that you may be able to endure it" (1 Cor 10:12-13).

In this life we might lack wisdom, but we never lack an Advocate. Our unfailing union with Christ is the grounds of our Christian living and thus of our prayer for wisdom. We can seek wisdom, because Wisdom sought us first. We can cry out for wisdom, because Wisdom summoned us first.

THE WISDOM OF THE CROSS

It is the pleasure of God to show the arrogance and foolishness of the worldly wise. Spiritual understanding is something granted, not something innately conjured. And when it comes to the ministry of the Lord Jesus, those whom others thought learned and wise were some of the very people to reject Christ and declare him a blasphemer. Jesus laments that not everyone repents in towns where he performed many mighty deeds (Mt 11:20-24).

But not everyone remains unrepentant. There are people who have faith in him and follow him. About them, Jesus prays,

> I thank you, Father, Lord of heaven and earth, that you have hidden these things from the wise and understanding and revealed them to little children; yes, Father, for such was your gracious will. All things have been handed over to me by my Father, and no one knows the Son except the Father, and

no one knows the Father except the Son and anyone to whom the Son chooses to reveal him. (Mt 11:25-27)

In Matthew 11:25, "the wise and understanding" is an ironic phrase. The "wise and understanding" are deemed such by the world, but when it comes to the truth about Jesus' person and work, the intelligent need an access and an insight that their learning cannot provide. They are dependent on the Son's sovereign will (Mt 11:27). The "little children" who know the Son are more than literal children. The phrase probably refers to those who, whether children or adults, have faith in Christ and yet might simultaneously be excluded by others for one reason or another. After all, children were not viewed highly in the ancient world. Surprisingly, then, the "children" are those who have come to know the Son, and the worldly wise are the ones in the spiritual dark.

The spiritual darkness of fools is on full display when religious leaders demand the death of Jesus, and crowds of supporters echo the demand by yelling, "Let him be crucified" (Mt 27:22-23). The apostles will later indict the people in Jerusalem for such malice. Peter says, "Men of Israel, hear these words: Jesus of Nazareth, a man attested to you by God with mighty works and wonders and signs that God did through him in your midst, as you yourselves know—this Jesus, delivered up according to the definite plan and foreknowledge of God, you crucified and killed by the hands of lawless men" (Acts 2:22-23).

The cross was at the same time the malice of people and the foreordained plan of God. A work of salvation was taking place despite the appearances of rejection and gore and agony. Humiliation would lead to exaltation. Accusation would lead to vindication. Suffering would lead to glory. Death would lead to life.

According to Romans 5:8, God demonstrated his love in the death of Christ, as the Son of God died in the place of sinners. But the cross was also an expression of the wisdom of God. This truth is a key feature of Paul's words to the Corinthians. In a culture enamored with worldly power and impressed by skill and persuasive rhetoric, Paul knew the Corinthians needed the forceful reminder that their salvation did not rest on the wisdom of man. He says,

"My speech and my message were not in plausible words of wisdom, but in demonstration of the Spirit and of power, so that your faith might not rest in the wisdom of men but in the power of God" (1 Cor 2:4-5).

The wisdom of the cross ensures that humanity has no grounds for boasting other than in the merciful work of God. Christ commissioned Paul to preach the gospel, which is the power of salvation for Jews and Gentiles (Rom 1:16). This message about the cross is "folly to those who are perishing" but "to us who are being saved it is the power of God" (1 Cor 1:18). Though the message of the cross provokes sinful ears, those who believe the message have only God to bless and praise for their spiritual sight.

The reason people perceive the cross as either folly or the power of God is God's plan to destroy "the wisdom of the wise" and to thwart "the discernment of the discerning" (1 Cor 1:19, quoting Is 29:14). Because the religious and political elites rejected and crucified Christ, God made their alleged wisdom look like foolishness. Crucifixion itself looked like humiliation and folly, yet through this foolishness God accomplished salvation. Truly, "the foolishness of God is wiser than men, and the weakness of God is stronger than men" (1 Cor 1:25). The cross was a picture of weakness, yet divine power was at work. A crucifixion was a scene of utter humiliation, yet Jesus now has the name above every name.

Given the power of the gospel and given that the message of the gospel centers on the mighty cross, Paul tells the Corinthians, "I decided to know nothing among you except Jesus Christ and him crucified" (1 Cor 2:2). Paul did not need a message impressive to the world when he already had a message that was saving the world.

As a believer in the "foolish" gospel, Paul was not preoccupied with being impressive to outsiders—or even to believers, for that matter. He did not want the Corinthians to be unduly influenced by worldly standards and strategies either. He says, "Consider your calling, brothers: not many of you were wise according to worldly standards, not many were powerful, not many were of noble birth" (1 Cor 1:26). According to worldly standards, the Corinthian saints would have been considered weak and lowly. Yet God chose the weak and the lowly to shame the strong and lofty (1 Cor 1:27-28).

Not only did Paul believe in the gospel about a Messiah who suffered, but he also suffered as he preached the gospel about this Messiah. Paul's suffering made him look weak in the eyes of others, but he accepted this outcome at a deeply theological level. He says, "If I must boast, I will boast of the things that show my weakness" (2 Cor 11:30). As Paul drew attention to his weakness, he knew God's strength would be displayed and thus God alone would be worthy of praise and boasting. Paul says, "I will boast all the more gladly of my weaknesses, so that the power of Christ may rest upon me. For the sake of Christ, then, I am content with weaknesses, insults, hardships, persecutions, and calamities. For when I am weak, then I am strong" (2 Cor 12:9-10).

Divine power displayed on the platform of weakness—*that* is the wisdom of God at work through the proclamation of the gospel and through those who proclaim it. Neither Paul nor the Corinthians—nor any of us—need to be preoccupied with the world being impressed by us. Our message bears the offense of the cross, which is a stumbling block to Jews and folly to Gentiles (1 Cor 1:18). Our focus should be holding to the gospel and keeping in step with its message.

Keeping in step with the gospel will mean bearing the fruit of the Spirit. It will mean wisdom, but not the wisdom of the world. Living in light of the gospel will mean receiving the wisdom of heaven.

CONCLUSION

To see the urgency of wisdom for our Christian lives, we need to know the kind of days we are living in. Under the sun, these days are evil, marked by corruption and rebellion and falsehood. Because of our union with Christ, we have put off the old self and have put on the new self—the Lord Jesus Christ. Even now the Holy Spirit is renewing and restoring us to be faithful image bearers who exercise dominion over sin and self.

We should pray for wisdom, that we might bear the fruit of the Spirit as we work out our salvation with fear and trembling. The "fear of the Lord" is not just an Old Testament concept. We are called to walk in reverence for Christ, holding fast to the gospel and being willing to face the misunderstanding of the self-assured, worldly wise. The gospel that causes them offense is nevertheless the gospel that saves from sin and makes new creations out of condemned sinners.

    The lordship of Christ over our lives is good news. We will grow in wisdom because God will bring to completion what he has begun in us. There are trials and sufferings to face, but God grants his people wisdom from above, wisdom found in Christ. There is no true wisdom apart from Christ, and we need his wisdom in all the areas of our lives. His lordship has no limit. The Christian life is a life under the Son.

Chapter Twelve

THE END OF THE NARROW WAY

BIBLICAL WISDOM IS MAINLY CONCERNED with this earthly life. We need to fear the Lord, love our neighbors, be faithful image bearers, serve local churches, work with integrity, do what is just, make countless decisions that affect our lives and the lives of others, raise families, steward our finances and resources, and prepare for the inevitability of death.

But biblical wisdom is not only concerned with this earthly life. The presence of unseen realities and the promise of ultimate things—such as judgment and resurrection and eternal states—do not diminish the importance of wisdom but establish its importance even more. We are not accidental outcomes of random molecular combinations and progressions. God has ordered his world, and a wise life seeks to live skillfully in the world he has made. But the eyes of wisdom are not just focused on the way things are, for the way things are is not the way they will be.

The things to come should weigh heavily enough on our earthly perspective that they affect the way we think about life here and now. A wise life is strengthened by a firm hope. Hope for the future helps us walk wisely and persevere.

LIFE HERE AND NOW

Those who hear and build their lives on the words of Jesus are the wise, and they will not face the judgment of the wicked (Mt 7:24-27). Their future is life. But what of their present? When does the life for which they were made begin?

Believers are no longer dead in their sins and trespasses. God has made us alive in Christ Jesus (Eph 2:4-6). The Holy Spirit's regenerating work in the heart of the sinner means the inauguration of eternal life. Jesus says, "Truly, truly, I say to you, whoever hears my word and believes him who sent me has eternal life. He does not come into judgment, but has passed from death to life" (Jn 5:24).

The sinner's regeneration is the passing from death to life. A new spiritual state exists, and we can call it "eternal life" even though the body will die. Though outwardly we waste away, inwardly we are being renewed day by day (2 Cor 4:16). This inner life is what Jesus means when he promises that those who believe in him will not perish (Jn 3:16). Because believers are in Christ, they are forever secure from condemnation. Christ is their righteousness.

A noncontradictory tension exists between the eternal life that begins inwardly and the bodily life that takes place at the resurrection of the dead. We really are new, even though we really will die. We live in the midst of a crooked generation, and we need to shine as lights in the world (Phil 2:15). This notion of shining is an allusion to Daniel 12:3, where the prophet is told that the "wise shall shine like the brightness of the sky above; and those who turn many to righteousness, like the stars forever and ever." In the context of Daniel 12, the heavenly being is talking about bodily resurrection and future glory. When we are in Christ, this shining is inaugurated.

The wise shine even now. The light of the Son shines through them and causes them to be lights in the world (Mt 5:14). The wise shine by holding to the truth. Paul says they are "holding fast to the word of life, so that in the day of Christ I may be proud that I did not run in vain or labor in vain" (Phil 2:16). The "word of life" is the gospel, the wise shine by holding to it, and holding to it involves both confession and conduct.

The crooked and twisted generation (both Paul's and ours) in Philippians 2:15 needs the light of the wise because the wise represent Christ and proclaim the word of life. This shining (by holding to the word of life) is connected to Paul's earlier point in Philippians 2:12, where he tells us to "work out your own salvation with fear and trembling." In the fear of the Lord, then, we hold to the word of life and shine as lights in the world.

But, of course, our present shining is only an inauguration of the life we were made to enjoy and embody. Greater glory is still to come, at the end of the narrow way.

THE PATH OF LIFE AND TO LIFE

The wise are on the path of life. To be more specific, it is the path *to* life. Jesus tells his listeners, "Enter by the narrow gate. For the gate is wide and the way is easy that leads to destruction, and those who enter by it are many. For the gate is narrow and the way is hard that leads to life, and those who find it are few" (Mt 7:13-14).

Think about how important the notion of destination is in Proverbs. The reason the father cautions his son away from Lady Folly is where her words will take him. Wickedness is spiritually hazardous not only because of what it does to the conscience and heart of the image bearer but also because of where it leads. Rebellion against the Lord leads to death.

When Jesus holds before his listeners a way "that leads to destruction" and a way "that leads to life," he is presenting the same binary as Proverbs. The wise are those who ponder where a road leads and who choose what is best, what is life giving. Only the narrow way leads to life, and only the wise will go through that gate.

The promise of unending life corresponds to communion with an eternal God who is the source of all life. To know and dwell with God is to experience a life derived from him. Given the kind of God he is, the life we receive from him is eternal. This kind of life is pictured in Psalm 1, where the wise person is "like a tree planted by streams of water that yields its fruit in its season, and its leaf does not wither. In all that he does, he prospers" (Ps 1:3). The congregation of the righteous will flourish in the presence of God, but the wicked shall blow away like chaff and perish under his judgment (Ps 1:4-6).

Jesus tells John in a vision, "But as for the cowardly, the faithless, the detestable, as for murderers, the sexually immoral, sorcerers, idolaters, and all liars, their portion will be in the lake that burns with fire and sulfur, which is the second death" (Rev 21:8). That list of vices could appear under a category labeled "folly." According to the Lord Jesus, there will be no foolishness in the new creation. No rebellion or unbelief. No idolatry or wickedness.

At the end of the narrow way is the new Jerusalem, the city of God. There will be no temple in the city, nor will there be any need for light, for the glory of God will be the light of his new creation (Rev 21:22-23). The path to everlasting life is the path to everlasting light, and the living God is the source of both. Christ says he gives "the light of life" to all who follow him (Jn 8:12). This light will never go out because our union with Christ can never dissolve.

EYES FOR UNSEEN THINGS

Since the wise have such a blessed future, they know how to live with hope. They have eyes that peer through the veil, seeing by faith the things God has promised for his people. The wise are like the patriarchs who died in faith,

> not having received the things promised, but having seen them and greeted them from afar, and having acknowledged that they were strangers and exiles on the earth. For people who speak thus make it clear that they are seeking a homeland. If they had been thinking of that land from which they had gone out, they would have had opportunity to return. But as it is, they desire a better country, that is, a heavenly one. Therefore God is not ashamed to be called their God, for he has prepared for them a city. (Heb 11:13-16)

The wise are heavenly minded. Does this mean they are no earthly good? By no means. C. S. Lewis puts it well:

> A continual looking forward to the eternal world is not (as some modern people think) a form of escapism or wishful thinking, but one of the things a Christian is meant to do. It does not mean that we are to leave the present world as it is. If you read history you will find that the Christians who did most for the present world were just those who thought most of the next.[1]

Heavenly mindedness clarifies our vision for this world, that we might live wisely and be less encumbered by the traps of worldliness. To be in the world

---

[1] C. S. Lewis, *Mere Christianity* (New York: Touchstone, 1980), 119.

but not of the world, we need eyes for what is unseen. Paul knew that believers would still suffer under the sun, but these afflictions serve a larger purpose: "For this light momentary affliction is preparing for us an eternal weight of glory beyond all comparison, as we look not to the things that are seen but to the things that are unseen. For the things that are seen are transient, but the things that are unseen are eternal" (2 Cor 4:17-18).

Meditating on eternal things helps us handle earthly things because this reflection orients our hearts. Paul says, "If then you have been raised with Christ, seek the things that are above, where Christ is, seated at the right hand of God. Set your minds on things that are above, not on things that are on earth. For you have died, and your life is hidden with Christ in God. When Christ who is your life appears, then you also will appear with him in glory" (Col 3:1-4).

By telling us to set our minds on the things that are above, Paul is not compromising the way of wisdom. He is showing us that true and biblical wisdom involves a mindset, a heart posture, that is informed by unseen and future realities. This connection is evident because he immediately says, "Put to death therefore what is earthly in you" (Col 3:5). Meditating on future glories can weaken the appeal of sin's lies and its bankrupt promises.

The wise know what to hope for. They know that a surpassing weight of glory is theirs in Christ. And they know that no earthly afflictions and no lies from Lady Folly will stop God from keeping all of his promises.

EMBODIED IMMORTALITY

An unseen reality that comprises our Christian hope is our bodily resurrection from the dead. Though our outer self is wasting away (2 Cor 4:16), we shall be raised in an eternal bodily dwelling (2 Cor 5:1-5). This mortal body will put on immortality (1 Cor 15:54). Think of our future resurrection as an embodied immortality, a glorified bodily life.

Glorified bodily life is what we were made for, as we can see from Genesis 2–3. God had planted two trees in the midst of the Garden of Eden: the tree of life and the tree of the knowledge of good and evil. When Adam and Eve ate from the forbidden tree, God prevented access to the tree of life (Gen 3:22-24). The knowledge of good and evil is about wisdom, yet eating what God had forbidden was an act of foolishness. Folly leads to exile, not to life.

In Christ, we have eternal life inaugurated. Because of our union with Christ, we will be raised bodily at his return. "For if we have been united with him in a death like his, we shall certainly be united with him in a resurrection like his" (Rom 6:5). The Lord's descent from heaven will mean the transformation of our lowly bodies to be like his glorious body (Phil 3:20-21). Think of our future resurrection as the fruit of the tree of life. In the last chapter of Scripture, we read about a river in the new creation, and on either side of the river is "the tree of life with its twelve kinds of fruit, yielding its fruit each month. The leaves of the tree were for the healing of the nations" (Rev 22:2).

In Christ, the fruit of the garden trees belongs to us. We know good and evil, and we have everlasting bodily life. By granting us such things, God is preparing us to reign in the new creation. We will receive the crown of life (Rev 2:10), and we shall reign with Christ forever (Rev 22:5). For now, "the wise die" (Ps 49:10). No matter how zealous believers may be for holiness, the body is outwardly wasting away, and to dust they shall return. But hear the hope of the psalmist: "God will ransom my soul from the power of Sheol, for he will receive me" (Ps 49:15).

Being ransomed from Sheol is resurrection. Being received into God's presence is everlasting life. The psalmist's hope becomes ours when the psalmist's refuge becomes ours—and his refuge is the living God. Death cannot abide in the presence of the Living One.

FOREVER TO BEHOLD

In Daniel 12:2-3, the promise is that the wise will rise and shine, and this glorified bodily life will never end. They will awake "to everlasting life" (Dan 12:2). But the glory they shine is a glory they shall come to share, by grace. It is the glory of God, the Uncreated One, whose glory emits from his very nature. The saints will not become gods, but their glorified bodies shall testify visibly to God's gracious and transforming power on them.

As people whom God shall raise to reign with Christ, they shall behold their Savior in all his glory. "They will see his face, and his name will be on their foreheads. And night will be no more. They will need no light of lamp or sun, for the Lord God will be their light, and they will reign forever and ever" (Rev 22:4-5). This experience was foreshadowed in the ministry of Christ when he was transfigured on a mountain in front of a few disciples. According to Luke's Gospel, "the appearance of his face was altered, and his clothing became dazzling white" (Lk 9:29). In Mark's Gospel, his radiant clothes were "intensely white, as no one on earth could bleach them" (Mk 9:3). In Matthew's Gospel, "his face shone like the sun, and his clothes became white as light" (Mt 17:2). Peter, James, and John temporally beheld the transfigured face and glory of Christ, and this was a preview of the unending glory and communion they would have with the Savior. Their brief experience will be our unending portion.

The Old Testament authors report a desire to behold the glory of God. Moses tells the Lord, "Please show me your glory" (Ex 33:18). David says, "As for me, I shall behold your face in righteousness; when I awake, I shall be satisfied with your likeness" (Ps 17:15). Moses and David's desires are clear: they wanted to behold the Lord. Who shall join them in this desire and in this experience? According to David, "the upright shall behold his face" (Ps 11:7).

The "upright" are the righteous, not the wicked. They are the wise, not the foolish. The upright trust the Lord, fear the Lord, and obey the Lord. The upright, then, will behold the One they fear. This beholding is sometimes called the beatific vision—the "happy" or "blessed" vision.[2] This vision corresponds to the God who is beheld, for he is "the blessed God" (1 Tim 1:11), "the blessed and only Sovereign" (1 Tim 6:15).

Forever beholding the Blessed One, the wise shall be forever blessed. The wise walk, for now, by faith and not by sight. But sight is coming. With a glorified body and soul, the wise will delight in infinite majesty, boundless joy, and incomprehensible beauty. David tells the Lord, "You make known to me the path of life; in your presence there is fullness of joy; at your right hand are pleasures forevermore" (Ps 16:11).

---

[2]For more on the beatific vision and the glory we will behold, see Samuel G. Parkison, *Irresistible Beauty: Beholding Triune Glory in the Face of Jesus Christ*, Reformed, Exegetical and Doctrinal Studies (Glasgow: Mentor, 2022); Patrick Schreiner, *The Transfiguration of Christ: An Exegetical and Theological Reading* (Grand Rapids, MI: Baker Academic, 2024).

The "path of life" is desirable for the wise because it is the path that leads to life with God. No other path has this destination. At the end of the narrow way is the beatific vision, and this end is at the same time a new beginning. The former things will have passed away, and new things, as well as unending delights, will be the moment-by-moment experience of the saints.

Who can fathom such a life? Who can begin to grasp the unsearchable riches that God has in store for his people? Who can imagine an end that is better than the beginning?

CONCLUSION

The life God has made us for is not entirely future. Something has begun now in us, by the work of the Holy Spirit. We are secure in our union with Christ because the life we have in him is eternal. Spiritually, we have been brought to life. Physically, we shall be raised to an embodied immortality when Christ returns.

The believer has a stabilizing hope in a world of uncertainties. By setting our minds on the things above, we will be orienting our hearts in the midst of disorienting temptations and afflictions under the sun. The direction of our lives is down the narrow way, and we will not fail to reach where it leads. It leads to a weight of glory surpassing all comparison. We shall be raised immortal, and with glorified sight we shall behold our redeemer in the city of God.

Isaiah says, "Your eyes will behold the king in his beauty; they will see a land that stretches afar" (Is 33:17). Only the wise will dwell with the king in a land that is fairer than day. Only the wise will shine like the stars of heaven. They have this hope because they walk the narrow way, and it is not the way to death. It is the way to life. When Christ returns, the wise will see that the end of the narrow way is a new kind of beginning. It will be "Chapter One of the Great Story which no one on earth has read: which goes on forever: in which every chapter is better than the one before."[3]

---

[3] C. S. Lewis, *The Last Battle*, Chronicles of Narnia (New York: HarperCollins, 1956), 228.

DISCUSSION GUIDE

1. How do the two central trees in the Garden of Eden relate to wisdom and folly?
2. How does Genesis 1:28 connect to a life of wisdom?
3. How is the concept of wisdom present in the book of Job?
4. What does it mean for Christians to fear the Lord?
5. What is the relationship between wisdom and obedience?
6. How does Israel's journey from Egypt to the Promised Land show wisdom and folly?
7. How should we understand Proverbs in light of the person and work of Christ?
8. What does the Song of Songs contribute to the notion of living wisely for God's glory?
9. How is the life of Solomon a testimony to both wisdom and folly?
10. Why is it helpful to think of the nation of Israel as a corporate Adam and son of God?
11. What Old Testament characters do you think exhibit, though imperfectly, a life of wisdom?

12. What Old Testament characters do you think demonstrate profound foolishness?
13. How does wisdom show up in the life and ministry of Jesus?
14. Why is a wise person concerned with the bigger picture and long-term outcomes?
15. How does the book of Revelation portray the consummation of a wise life?

SCRIPTURE INDEX

OLD TESTAMENT

Genesis
1, *8, 18, 86*
1–2, *91*
1–3, *14, 19*
1–11, *19*
1:4, *8*
1:9, *8*
1:9-10, *8*
1:11-12, *8*
1:20, *8*
1:22, *8*
1:25, *10*
1:26, *7, 8, 143*
1:27, *7, 143*
1:28, *8, 14, 17, 74, 143*
2, *10, 13, 65, 76, 90*
2–3, *159*
2:7, *90*
2:8, *9*
2:9, *83, 90*

2:15, *9*
2:16-17, *9, 11, 90*
2:17, *90*
2:20-23, *10*
2:25, *13*
3, *10, 11, 12, 13, 15, 17, 28, 34, 55, 65, 83, 90, 106, 115*
3:1, *11, 12, 23*
3:2-3, *11*
3:3, *11*
3:4, *12, 126*
3:4-5, *11*
3:5, *11, 12, 13, 28*
3:6, *12, 17, 55*
3:7, *12, 13, 17*
3:8, *13*
3:9, *15*
3:10, *13, 15, 17*
3:12-13, *13*
3:14-19, *13*
3:15, *16, 20*

3:16, *96*
3:16-19, *17*
3:17, *106*
3:19, *106*
3:20, *14*
3:22, *13, 83*
3:22-24, *33, 90, 159*
3:24, *14*
4, *15, 26*
4:1-4, *14*
4:4, *26*
4:6-7, *14, 15*
4:8, *15*
4:9, *15*
4:23-24, *16*
4:25, *16*
4:26, *16*
5, *16, 22*
5:1, *143*
5:21-23, *16*
5:22, *16*
5:24, *16*

5:28-31, *16*
5:29, *16, 20*
6, *17*
6–8, *99*
6:1-4, *17*
6:2, *17*
6:5, *17*
6:7, *17*
6:11-12, *17*
7:11-24, *17*
9, *18*
9:1, *17*
9:22, *17*
9:23, *17*
9:25, *18*
9:26-27, *18*
11, *18, 19, 22*
11:1-9, *19*
11:3, *18*
11:4, *18, 19*
11:7, *19*
11:9, *19*
11:30, *33*
12, *34*
12:1, *33*
12:2-3, *33*
12:7, *33*
12:11-13, *34*
14:13-16, *34*
15, *34*
15:4, *33*
15:5, *33*
15:6, *33*
16, *34*
16:2, *34*
17:6, *56*
18:12-15, *34*
21:6, *34*
37, *35*
37–50, *123*
37:25-28, *35*

39, *35*
39:3-6, *37*
39:10, *35*
39:11-20, *35*
39:21-22, *37*
39:21-23, *35*
40, *36*
41:8, *36*
41:14, *36*
41:38, *123*
41:39, *36*
41:40, *36*
42–44, *36*
45, *37*
45:4-5, *37*
49, *56*
49:10, *56, 59, 62*
50:20, *37*

Exodus
1, *37*
1:15-21, *56*
1:16, *37*
1:17, *38, 39*
1:19, *39*
1:20, *39*
1:20-21, *38*
1:21, *39*
2:2, *39*
2:3-5, *39*
2:6-9, *39*
2:10, *39*
3, *99*
3:8, *96*
4:22, *41, 77, 121*
12:37-38, *40*
13:21-22, *40*
14, *99*
14:11-12, *40*
14:12, *40*
14:21-22, *40*
14:27-29, *40*

14:31, *40*
15:26, *41*
19, *42, 98*
20, *42*
20:1-17, *45*
20:12, *133*
21–23, *42*
23:33, *42*
24, *99*
24:3, *42*
24:6-7, *42*
24:8, *42, 96*
32, *43*
32:1-6, *43*
32:27-29, *43*
32:35, *43*
33:18, *161*
34:12, *43*

Leviticus
10:1-3, *26*
26, *52*

Numbers
3:7-8, *9*
8:26, *9*
10, *43*
11, *43*
11:1, *43*
11:4-5, *43*
11:4-6, *43*
11:6, *43*
13–14, *43*
13:28, *43*
13:31, *44*
14:1-2, *44*
14:4, *44*
14:11, *44*
14:29, *44*
14:33-34, *44*
18:5-6, *9*

Scripture Index

Deuteronomy
1, *81*
4:5-6, *47*
4:6-8, *54*
5:6-21, *45*
5:7, *46*
6, *81*
6:5, *45, 46, 81*
6:6, *45*
6:6-7, *81*
6:10-12, *45*
6:13, *46*
6:13-14, *46*
8:2, *46, 54*
8:5-6, *82*
8:6, *47*
11:9, *82*
11:17, *82*
17, *59, 118*
17:14-20, *75, 77, 128*
17:16-17, *57, 118*
17:18-20, *57*
17:19, *57*
17:19-20, *119*
28, *52*
28:63-64, *121*
30:15, *47*
30:19-20, *47*
34:9, *50*
34:10-12, *50*

Joshua
1:8, *51*
1:16-17, *51*
2:18, *96*
10–12, *51*
23, *51*
23:6-8, *51*
23:11, *51*
23:14, *52*
23:15, *52*

24, *56*
24:2, *33*
24:14, *52*
24:16, *52*
24:18, *52*
24:19-20, *53*
24:31, *53*

Judges
2:10, *53*
2:11-12, *53*
2:14-15, *53*
2:23, *54*
3:4, *54*
3:7, *54*
17:6, *55, 56*
18:1, *55, 56*
19:1, *55, 56*
21:25, *55, 56*

1 Samuel
8, *58, 59*
8:5, *58*
8:6, *59*
8:7, *58, 59*
8:10-18, *59*
8:18, *59*
8:19, *59*
8:20, *58*
9:1-2, *59*
12:14-15, *59*
12:19, *59*
12:20-21, *59*
12:24, *59*
12:25, *59*
13:8-10, *59*
13:13, *60*
14:29, *60*
15:18-19, *60*
16, *61*
17:31-37, *62*

18–26, *62*
19:1, *60*
22:21, *60*
28:7-8, *60*

2 Samuel
5, *62*
7, *63, 64*
7:12-13, *63, 127, 131*
7:16, *63*
11–12, *62*
23, *62, 63, 64*
23:1-4, *62*
23:4, *63*
23:5-7, *63*

1 Kings
1–11, *75, 131*
2:2-3, *75*
3–10, *117*
3:5, *75*
3:9, *75*
3:11-12, *134*
3:12, *75*
3:16-27, *75*
3:28, *75*
4, *75*
4:20, *75*
4:25, *76*
4:29-31, *75*
4:32, *76, 90*
4:33, *76*
4:34, *76*
5:7, *76*
10, *135*
10:1, *76, 135*
10:2, *135*
10:3, *76*
10:6-7, *76, 135*
10:10, *135*
10:14-29, *118*

10:26-27, *118*
10:28, *118*
11:1-2, *118*
11:3, *118*
11:3-4, *119*
11:4, *118*
11:5, *118*
11:6, *118*
11:7, *118*
11:9, *118*
11:10, *119*
11:11-13, *119*
11:31, *119*
12:4, *119*
12:8, *119*
12:10-11, *119*
12:13-14, *119*
12:16-20, *119*
14:22-24, *120*

2 Kings
17, *120*
17:7-9, *120*
17:13, *121*
23:27, *121*

2 Chronicles
1–9, *75*
2:12, *76*
9:5-6, *76*

Job
1:1, *22, 27, 30*
1:2, *23*
1:3, *22, 23*
1:5, *23, 30*
1:6-7, *23*
1:8, *23*
1:9-10, *23*
1:10-11, *30*
1:11, *23*

1:13-19, *24*
1:21, *24, 30*
1:22, *25*
2:3, *24*
2:4-5, *24*
2:7, *24*
2:7-8, *24*
2:9, *24*
2:10, *24, 25*
2:11, *25, 29*
2:12-13, *25*
2:13, *25, 29*
3:3-4, *29*
4:7-9, *25*
4:8, *25*
8:4, *25*
11:3, *25*
11:6, *25*
12:13, *25*
13:3, *25*
13:12, *26*
27:5-6, *27*
28, *27*
28:12, *27*
28:13, *27*
28:23, *27*
28:27, *27*
28:28, *27*
38–41, *27, 28*
38:2-3, *28*
40:4-5, *28*
42:2, *28*
42:5-6, *28*
42:16, *22*

Psalms
1–2, *64, 65*
1:1, *24, 66*
1:1-2, *140*
1:2, *65, 69*
1:3, *65, 157*

1:4-6, *140, 157*
1:6, *140*
2:1-3, *65*
2:2, *65*
2:3, *65*
2:6, *67*
2:7, *66*
2:10-12, *65*
2:12, *66*
9, *64*
10, *64*
11:7, *161*
15:1, *67*
15:2-3, *67*
15:4, *67*
16:11, *161*
17:15, *161*
19:7, *69*
19:10, *69*
23:1-3, *68*
23:2, *138*
23:4-5, *68*
23:6, *68*
24:3, *67*
24:4-5, *67*
24:7, *67*
25:4-5, *69*
25:8-10, *70*
25:9, *70*
25:12, *70*
25:14, *70*
26:1-3, *71*
26:4-5, *71*
27:11, *71*
34:8-9, *71*
34:11-14, *72*
41:11-12, *72*
49:10, *160*
49:15, *160*
51, *62*

Scripture Index

Proverbs
1, *84*
1–9, *77, 78*
1:1, *78, 103*
1:1-7, *78*
1:2-6, *78*
1:4, *80*
1:7, *78, 79*
1:8, *132*
1:15-16, *80*
1:18, *80*
1:20-21, *84*
1:23, *85, 137*
1:24, *85*
1:26-28, *85*
1:29, *79*
1:33, *85, 137*
2:3, *149*
2:5, *79*
2:6, *150*
2:7, *81*
2:8, *81*
2:16, *85*
2:18-19, *85*
2:19, *83*
2:21-22, *82*
3:1, *81*
3:1-8, *122*
3:5, *81*
3:5-6, *81*
3:11-12, *82, 148*
3:12, *147*
3:14-15, *85*
3:15, *85*
3:16, *85*
3:16-18, *137*
3:17, *83, 85*
3:18, *83, 84*
3:19-20, *8*
4:6-8, *85*
5, *35*
5:5-6, *85*

5:6, *83*
5:8, *85*
5:20, *35*
6:6, *79*
6:10-11, *87*
7:4-5, *85*
7:25-27, *85*
8, *86, 138*
8:11, *85*
8:13, *79*
8:22-23, *86, 138*
8:22-31, *86*
8:24, *138*
8:24-31, *86*
8:35-36, *86*
9:5-6, *137*
9:10, *23, 38, 47, 57, 78, 79*
10–31, *79*
10:1, *132*
10:2, *87*
10:9, *86*
10:27, *79*
11:30, *83*
13:12, *83*
13:20, *113*
13:21, *87*
14:27, *79*
15:4, *83*
15:16, *79*
15:33, *79*
16:6, *79*
19:23, *79*
22:4, *79*
23:17, *79*
25:1, *77*
26:4-5, *42*
30–31, *77*
31:30, *78, 79*

Ecclesiastes
1:1, *103, 104*

1:1-11, *102*
1:2, *104, 105*
1:3, *106*
1:4, *105*
1:5-7, *105*
1:12, *104*
1:12–12:7, *103*
2–3, *108*
2:4-8, *104*
2:9, *104*
2:14, *106*
2:18-19, *105*
2:22, *106*
2:24-26, *108*
3, *108*
3:1, *106*
3:1-8, *107*
3:11, *107*
3:12-13, *108*
3:14, *115*
3:17, *114*
3:20, *106*
4:2, *102*
4:9-12, *113*
5:1, *104*
5:10, *109*
5:13-15, *110*
5:18, *110*
7:2, *111*
7:5, *113, 114*
7:13-14, *107*
7:18, *115*
8:12, *115*
8:15, *110*
8:17, *107*
9:10, *109*
11:4, *112*
11:9, *115*
12:1, *115*
12:8-14, *102*
12:9, *102, 103*

12:9-10, *103*
12:10, *103*
12:13, *114*
12:13-14, *114, 115*
12:14, *114*

Song of Solomon
1:1, *90, 103*
1:1–2:7, *91*
1:2-4, *91*
1:3, *92*
1:4, *96*
1:5, *96*
1:10, *92*
1:12-14, *96*
1:13, *92*
1:14, *92*
1:17, *92*
2:2-3, *92*
2:5, *91*
2:6, *91*
2:7, *93*
2:8-13, *91*
2:8–3:5, *91*
2:13, *96*
2:14, *92*
2:15, *92*
3:1-5, *92*
3:5, *93*
3:6, *91*
3:6–5:1, *91*
3:11, *91*
4:1-2, *96*
4:1–5:1, *96*
4:3, *96*
4:11, *96*
4:12, *96*
4:15, *96*
5:1, *96*
5:2–8:4, *91, 92*
5:10-16, *96*

6:2, *92*
7:1-9, *96*
7:10, *96*
8:4, *93*
8:5-14, *91*
8:6, *98*
8:7, *99*
8:8-9, *95*
8:13-14, *92*

Isaiah
5, *97*
5:1-2, *97*
5:1-7, *97*
5:7, *97*
9, *128*
9:2, *128*
9:6, *128*
9:6-7, *128*
11:1, *128*
11:2, *128, 132*
29:14, *152*
33:17, *162*
54:5, *96*

Jeremiah
2:2, *96*
3:8, *96*
14:15, *126*
31:31-34, *127*
31:32, *96*

Ezekiel
16:8, *96*

Daniel
1:3-4, *121*
1:8, *121*
1:17, *121*
1:19-20, *122*
2:1-2, *122*

2:7-11, *122*
2:20-23, *122*
2:31-45, *123*
2:46-49, *123*
2:48, *123*
3:17-18, *125*
4:18, *123*
4:27, *123*
4:29-30, *123*
4:37, *123*
6, *124*
6:3, *124*
6:4, *124*
6:5, *124*
6:7-9, *124*
6:10, *124*
6:16, *124*
6:20-22, *124*
11–12, *126*
11:32-35, *125, 126*
12, *156*
12:2, *125, 126, 160*
12:2-3, *160*
12:3, *126, 156*

Hosea
1:2, *96*
1:2–2:3, *96*
14:4-7, *127*
14:9, *127*

New Testament

Malachi
4, *130*

Matthew
1, *130*
1:1, *131*
1:2-16, *131*
1:19, *132*

Scripture Index

2, *135*
2:1, *135*
2:11, *135*
4:17, *135, 137*
4:19, *137*
5–7, *135*
5:14, *156*
5:17, *133*
6:24, *110*
6:33, *110*
7, *136*
7:13-14, *136, 140, 157*
7:19, *140*
7:21-23, *140*
7:24-27, *136, 139, 140, 156*
7:28-29, *136*
11:20-24, *150*
11:25, *151*
11:25-27, *151*
11:27, *151*
12, *134*
12:42, *134, 135*
13, *135*
13:9, *136*
17:2, *161*
21, *131*
21–22, *136*
21:9, *131*
22:22, *136*
22:37-38, *45*
26:25, *135*
26:30, *64*
27:22-23, *151*

Mark
1:11, *133*
1:14-15, *135*
1:27, *136*
2:8, *136*
4, *135*
4:11-12, *135*
9:3, *161*
10:17, *135*
10:47, *131*

Luke
1–2, *132*
1:26-38, *132*
1:38, *132*
2:1-20, *132*
2:21, *132*
2:22, *132*
2:22-38, *132*
2:39, *132*
2:40, *132, 133, 134*
2:41, *132*
2:41-52, *132*
2:46-47, *134*
2:46-49, *134*
2:49, *134*
2:50, *134*
2:51, *133*
2:52, *133, 134*
6, *135*
9:29, *161*

John
1, *138*
1:1-3, *138*
2:24-25, *136*
3:16, *156*
3:28-29, *95*
5:14, *26*
5:24, *156*
6, *135*
6:60-66, *139*
6:67, *139*
6:68-69, *139*
7:46, *136*
8:12, *137, 158*
10:14-16, *138*
14:6, *138, 140*

14:15, *47*
15:1, *144*
15:5, *144*
15:13, *71*
15:14, *71*
15:15, *71*
17, *100*
17:26, *100*

Acts
2:22-23, *151*
4, *64*
4:25, *64*
5:5-10, *26*
13:21, *59*

Romans
1–11, *144*
1:16, *152*
5:8, *151*
5:12-21, *90*
6:2-4, *145*
6:5, *160*
8:1, *144*
8:28, *108*
8:38-39, *98*
11:33, *107*
11:34, *107*
12–16, *144*
12:2, *143*

1 Corinthians
1:18, *152, 153*
1:19, *152*
1:25, *152*
1:26, *152*
1:27-28, *152*
1:30, *137*
2:2, *152*
2:4-5, *152*
10:12-13, *150*

10:31, *109*
11:29-30, *26*
15:54, *159*

2 Corinthians
4:16, *2, 156, 159*
4:17-18, *159*
4:17–5:5, *2*
5:1-5, *159*
5:17, *2, 145*
7:1, *146*
11:3, *23*
11:14, *23*
11:30, *153*
12:9-10, *153*

Galatians
2:20, *144*
5:19-21, *145*
5:22-23, *145*

Ephesians
1–3, *144*
2:4-6, *156*
4–6, *144*
4:18, *147*
4:22-24, *146*
4:23, *143*
4:24, *143*
4:25, *147*
4:26, *147*
4:28, *147*
4:29, *147*
5, *95*
5:1, *147*
5:8, *147*
5:10, *147*
5:11, *147*

5:15, *146*
5:15-16, *142, 148*
5:16, *142, 146*
5:17, *146*
5:18-21, *146*
5:22–6:9, *146*
5:32, *95*
6:1, *147*
6:2-3, *147*
6:4, *147*
6:12, *30*

Philippians
1:6, *2, 145*
1:9-11, *145*
2:12, *144, 157*
2:15, *156*
2:16, *156*
3:20-21, *160*

Colossians
2:3, *136*
3:1-4, *159*
3:5, *159*
3:9-10, *145*
3:10, *144*
4:5-6, *148*

1 Thessalonians
5:16-18, *109*

1 Timothy
1:11, *161*
4:7-8, *146*
4:12, *94*
5:2, *94*
6:8-10, *110*
6:15, *161*

2 Timothy
3:16, *102*

Titus
2:6, *94*

Hebrews
4:14-15, *150*
4:15, *132*
5:8, *132*
11:13-16, *158*
12:5-6, *148*
12:7-8, *147*
12:10-11, *148*
13:4, *92*

James
1:2-4, *149*
1:5, *149*
3:13, *149*
3:14-15, *149*
3:16, *149*
3:17, *148*
3:17-18, *148, 149*
4:14, *105*
5:11, *31*

Revelation
2:10, *160*
12:9, *23*
21:8, *158*
21:22-23, *158*
22:2, *160*
22:4-5, *161*
22:5, *160*